The Delphian Talks

The Delphian Talks
by Evelyn Rucker
Layout by Helane Freeman

Copyright © 2017 Doug Rucker
All rights reserved.

Doug Rucker
Vilimapubco
Malibu, CA
ruckerdoug@gmail.com

No part of this publication may be reproduced, distributed, or transmitted in any form or by any means, including photocopying, recording, or other electronic or mechanical methods, without the prior written permission of the publisher, except in the case of brief quotations embodied in critical reviews and certain other noncommercial uses permitted by copyright law.

For permission requests, sales to U.S. bookstores and wholesalers, or to inquire about quantity discounts, please contact the publisher at the email address above.

Printed in the United States of America

Library of Congress Control Number: 2017904937

ISBN 978-0-9968060-9-1

First Edition
10 9 8 7 6 5 4 3 2 1

The Delphian Talks

Evelyn Rucker

Table of Contents

Eulogy

Foreword

The Delphian Talks

    Lilacia Park (1984) 1

    Ancestral Ghosts (1985) 11

    Happiness Is? (1985) 37

    Irish Talk (1987) 53

    The Ralph Chaplin Story (1988) 75

    Where Do We Go From Here? (1989) 97

    Presidential Timber (1990) 113

    Tribute to Golden (1991) 125

    Florida Bound Vagabonds (1992) 139

Appendix

EULOGY

EVELYN MARIE COSTELLO RUCKER
(6/23/02 - 4/29/96)
(By eldest son, Douglas)

Mother died at 4:30 AM on April 29, 1996. She asked younger brother David and I to send her to Denver's Care Center so there would be nurse's available constantly to take care of her. She did quite well there for almost 10 months, but David suspected she was losing ground when he saw her weight chart. Though she had excellent care, still she only weighed seventy-eight pounds when she died.

During the last few months, her body was seriously failing and though she didn't seem in pain, yet she was never really comfortable. Dave thinks she may have become resolved enough that she was surreptitiously spitting out her medications.

She had talked about wanting to die for the past year or two. In 1993 she published an article in the Denver Post on Euthanasia and ended the article with:

"I'm weary. Oh, how wonderful it would be to call loved ones to a party, to say a happy goodbye, to have that pill administered, and then **to leave for possibly another adventure with grace and dignity.**

In the end, she didn't watch TV or talk to her roommate, nor did she participate in one of her favorite activities, reading.

Life was much too strenuous for her. She lived almost 94 years, till almost the twentieth century. And happily she died in her sleep.

I loved Mother very much. She was always kind to me and taught me many valuable things. In retrospect, I am pleased as expressed in her article she finally got her wish.

"...and then to leave for possibly another great adventure with grace and dignity."

My brother, Dave, saw her religiously twice a week while she was at the Care Center and cared for her as needed when she lived in her house on 23rd Street.

Boyd Barkey, her next-door neighbor, considered her like his own mother. He took out her trash, planted a garden on her property and shared vegetables and dropped in for coffee and friendly chats. Mother loved Boyd very much and called him her third son.

Mother was an enthusiastic member of the **Golden Garden Club**. She entered flower contests and participated in their beautiful displays and always had many wonderful things to say about the members. She even got me to design the cover for their monthly minutes.

She also adored the **Delphian Club,** which seemed to be made for just such a person as **Evelyn Rucker**, it being a social group of intellectual women who love the mind and sharing its ideas.

For nine years between 1983 and 1992 she gave the **Delphian** members a once-a-year hour-long talk on subjects the board suggested and that interested her. Some of my favorites were **Lilacia Park, The Ralph Chaplin Story** and **Florida Bound Vagabonds**.

I liked best the last one she composed called **Florida Bound Vagabonds**, since it is one of her oldest and most favorite stories. I suggested she write it down, for we agreed it would make a wonderful movie script.

The story is about **Evelyn** and her then good friend, **Phil**, driving from Chicago to Florida, chaperoned by her newly married younger sister and husband.

They sing along in the old Model T Ford car, sleep among the stars, get part time jobs, meet interesting people and have many adventures. Eventually, they get married in Florida. You'll love to read her story in her book called, ***The Delphian Talks***.

Mother was the oldest in a family of six. Her father, **E. J. Costello**, was a newspaperman and editor. He was a great influence on her life and she spoke of him with reverence until the end.

E.J. was a friend of H. L. Mencken, Damon Runyon, Gene Fowler, Clarence Darrow, and other interesting writers. Once, while interviewing Teddy Roosevelt, Teddy and my grandfather made the front page with a picture of Teddy, grabbing E. J.'s hat and donning it for his first ride in an open cockpit airplane. He was an intellectual idealist and considered mother his protégé. He encouraged her to keep a daily journal, read voraciously, and write.

Mother responded by becoming almost an obsessed reader. During her eighth year I have seen a record of the books she'd read. There were about fifty and included works by DeFoe, Dickens, Austen, Conrad, Poe, Melville, Twain, etc. Throughout her life, books educated her, stimulated her imagination, and provided inspiration. Reading was the way she spent her favorite time.

During school she showed a talent for writing. Embarrassed and shy, she was always asked to read her poems and stories to other classes. The teachers agreed she had a great gift that should not be wasted. Later she earned money writing for magazines and afterward contributed to local newspapers.

She also began a life-long diary, which Dave and I have inherited. I haven't finished all the 16, 1-1/2" to 3" loose-leaf binders in their entirety, but I've skimmed a few years and am interested to finish and find the details of my mother's life.

Mother lived to dance and for a while took lessons. During her office work with the Shonk's factory in Chicago, she choreographed dances for a dozen nymphets for the annual variety show. The production was a hit and we have pictures of this famous episode with she and her girls in costume on stage. We even have one picture of mother lying on her stomach with her leg bent backward and the bottom of her foot within a few inches of her head.

Her husband, **Phil Rucker**, was doing a comedy routine in the same show. Resembling Fred Astaire, he was an excellent dancer and very funny. Mother, shy and introverted, was intrigued with this funny, outgoing person. Eventually, they became a real love match and Phil became our much-loved dad.

Mother also loved music, mostly classical, and studied the piano for many years. Her favorite piece was Rachmaninoff's, Prelude in C-sharp minor, but she also liked Beethoven, Bach and Brahms. Over the radio, we listened regularly to the Chicago Symphonic Hour on Chicago's station WGN. It came on at twelve, noon, the exact time I was home for lunch from school.

Mother loved education and was especially instrumental in seeing that brother Dave and I went to College. Dave graduated in **music** from Drake University and I graduated in **architecture** from the University of Illinois. Following our chosen professions, we both consider ourselves successes and are working in them to this day.

Our blue-collar dad saw us through the great 1929 depression, but we had little extra money to spend. Mother and dad had to learn to be frugal and mother applied herself to this end. Because of this, I learned to live frugally without apology.

Mother didn't believe human worth was connected to material wealth, but she did believe we could have interior wealth through honesty, compassion, integrity, fairness, imagination, intelligence and diligence.

She was against any form of prejudice. When I made statements showing preliminary judgment of groups, mother would tell me about it. I am thankful she taught me this, because prejudice is cruel, boring, petty, dangerous and time consuming. I wish, like my mother, it didn't exist.

I am grateful I have included dance in my life. My lovely wife, Marge, is an accomplished dancer and has taught me most of what I know about dance.

I am grateful I love music the way I do. I sang in a Renaissance chorus group for nine years and have a big collection of jazz and classical music that I listen to while doing my architectural office work. Dave is an outstanding music teacher and works with a smaller group continuously doing gigs in the Denver musical scene.

I am grateful for mother's love of reading, for it has become a major part of my life, too. Because of it I am better educated. My imagination is working and I, too, am inspired.

Dave reads something even harder - a musical score.

I am grateful for my mother's love of writing. She influenced me to write a 400-page poetry book, thirteen short comedy books, an autobiography of 3 books, plus three more containing comedy, philosophy and psychology.

I am pleased I graduated from college. I have always been proud that I could do such a thing and it was also a source of pride for mother to know her two sons had completed that portion of their education.

I'm glad mother was an athletic person. Dave and I have enjoyed football, track, swimming, skating, baseball, basketball, running, springboard diving, surfing and skiing.

I have enjoyed mother for her philosophy and compassionate attitude toward life.

Her gifts have been extended to me and what's more, I have extended her gifts and my gifts to my three daughters and Dave to his son and daughter. Now our kids are having kids and these same values will continue. I am grateful.

Mother is not dead. She didn't go very far. She's still with us.

It is my hope she is on yet another - **great adventure.**

Douglas W. Rucker

FOREWORD

The following nine works are yearly talks given to *The Delphian Club* of Golden Colorado. They were written by my mother, Evelyn Rucker, during her eight-year membership.

Sending me one copy of each talk over the years in addition to her other writings and publications, my file on her works has grown to considerable size. To whittle the file-folder, then, and consolidate these unique efforts, I have organized her first book, *The Delphian Club* into this single volume.

These programs are reproduced unedited by me and it should be remembered they were written by my Mother to be *spoken aloud* rather than *for silent reading*. She had no chance to edit them herself, nor did I give her the chance, since this book is to be a surprise for her ninetieth birthday. I beg her forgiveness and hope she thinks well of me, even so.

I love these stories and have collected them for my personal enjoyment in reading and remembering over the years and to make mother's experiences, point of view, and style of telling easily accessible to those who also love her; sons and daughters-in-law, relatives and grand-children, great-grandchildren, friends, acquaintances, and all others who enjoy and benefit from life stories uniquely told.

Doug Rucker

THE DELPHIAN TALKS

I wish to quote from my mother's letter of April 21, 1992.

The Delphian Club was started by several women in the 1930's who had married professors at the Colorado School of Mines, but who hadn't had college educations.

They had known of the Delphian Society in Chicago, which provided material for higher education by mail. Several signed up for the courses, which cost over a hundred dollars for the books, and decided to meet weekly in the mornings from 9:30 AM until noon and study.

One hundred dollars was a lot of money to spend on education in the 1930's, but they persisted and many got their degrees.

Our Delphian's is a social more than a study club, but each member must do one program during the season from September until April. We terminate with a fancy luncheon in May with a guest speaker. This year it will be at a very nice restaurant in Golden.

The programs herein are those given by my mother to the Delphian Club over an eight-year period from 1984 to 1992.

Doug Rucker

LILAC PARK
Lombard, Illinois

Once upon a time, many years ago during my adolescence, our family moved to a delightful small town called Lombard. It was about twenty miles west of the great metropolis of Chicago and set in the midst of lush farmlands. Our home was on a five-acre tract at the end of a cul-de-sac on Columbine Avenue. This was the last street in town but there were good neighbors and soon we became part of an interesting community.

*Paul, Helen, John, Marguerite, Evelyn Costello.
Lombard, Illinois (1918)*

This was a completely new experience for us children for we had always lived in rented houses in cities to which my father had usually been transferred because of his work as a newspaper correspondent. Finally, it looked as if we would be in the Chicago area more or less permanently so it was time to buy a place.

Father wasn't the most practical man in the world and was something of a dreamer. He had read with great interest Thorstein Veblen's book, *Three Acres and Freedom*, and was idealist enough to believe that he could settle his family on acreage, work as a commuter on the Northwestern to the city, raise our own food, and provide the best surroundings for his growing family.

Other newsmen, artists, and novelists must have had the same dream for they had planted their families in that area also. It became, in fact, to use the term in vogue in the twenties, quite a *"Bohemian"* settlement. Carl Sandberg, then Labor Editor on the Chicago Daily News, lived in nearby Elmhurst, and Father often rode to work on the train with him. Harold Grey, creator of the comic strip, *Little Orphan Annie*, came with his ailing young wife to live on Main Street with his parents to help her recuperate on their wide sun porch. She died later and sometime afterward he married Virginia Frost who was our neighbor.

Newsmen Howard Mann and Charles Michaels lived with their families in Lombard, and poet and painter, Ralph Chaplin, and his artist wife were our neighbors, as well as novelist and magazine writer, Katherine Reynolds and family, one of whose sons, Tom, shared my home and memories for a while. Colonel and Mrs. William R. Plum were perhaps the most esteemed residents in Lombard. They occupied a large home set on two and a half acres near the center of town. The Colonel had served at age 17 as a volunteer telegrapher under the command of General George R. Thomas in the Civil War. Afterward, he worked on night duty as a telegraph operator in New Haven while attending Yale to study law. He graduated in 1867, married Helen M. Williams, direct descendent of Roger Williams, and established himself in law offices in Chicago. Around that time he bought the home in Lombard, which was to become the nucleus of Lilacia Park.

The Plums had traveled a great deal, especially after he retired, and had visited all forty-eight states in the Union as well as many countries in Europe and Asia. Their great interest in lilacs started with a trip to the famous lilac gardens in Lemoine, France in 1911. There they bought their first two treasures, the lovely pure white Madame Casimer Perrier, and a double light purple called the Michael Buchner. They loved trees as well and often brought home such beauties as my favorite, the giant Schwedler Maple, in all its red glory, from the Black Forest in Germany.

The couple had no children but they were generous and civic minded, and their home was often thrown open for local gatherings and cultural affairs of many sorts. They were already very elderly when we arrived in town and Mrs. Plum died soon after. The Colonel followed her in 1927, at age 82, and in lieu of direct heirs and mindful of his love for his favorite village, bequeathed his estate to Lombard for a park. The home was designated as the Helen M. Plum Library in honor of his wife. It always had been filled with books. Eventually a park district was set up in this village of about 3,000 inhabitants then, and the old carriage house was cleared and turned into an Administration Building. Famous landscape artist, Jens Jensen, was hired. He had planned many of the Chicago Parks and Conservatories, and was considered the *"dean of world landscape architects".* Many times he had received as much as $100,000 for his fee, but in this depression time, he charged only $600 for this work, and it became a favorite.

Now the time had arrived to make this little gem known to the public. All of us thought that this great beauty should be shared. In April 1929, my father, E. J. Costello, was invited to address the Lion's Club on the subject. He outlined the possibilities of publicizing this fabulous collection and putting Lombard on the map as Lilac Town. His talk generated much enthusiasm, and he promised that he and other newsmen and artists in the area would contribute their efforts. He suggested a Lilac Queen, pageant, a parade, etc. The merchants excitedly imagined their town becoming famous in the manner of Pasadena with its Rose Parade!

Before the summer was over, a beehive of activity had been set into motion. The original estate was augmented by several acres; Jens Jensen began laying out paths, setting bushes back along them to make room for wide borders of brilliant tulips from Holland, as they would bloom at Lilac Time. Lombard artist, Charles Medin, drew a beautiful lilac poster, which was printed and also used for car stickers. His brother-in-law, Ralph Chaplin, wrote a poem about Lilac Time in Lombard. The newsmen got busy and wrote glowing stories of Lombard's treasure for their Chicago papers, and they gave them wide and favorable coverage. May 17 was set as a target date (for lilac blooms were iffy), and Clara Bauman Petee began to write the first pageant, which she would direct herself

In the spring of 1930, a popularity contest among Lombard girls for queen was launched, and ballots were placed in all stores to sell for a nickel apiece, as money was much needed in this severe depression time. The local thespian group began work on their production of *"The Green Goddess",* a then popular play, to help. The special talents of all of the townspeople were solicited, and committees were set up for finance, music, dance, publicity, costumes, queen contest, etc. Nearly every family was involved in some way. Many donated pieces of old silver, silver spoons, pins, etc., to be melted down. And, of course, Christia Reade, artist daughter of early settler Josiah Reade, designed and executed a lovely crown to be passed from queen to future queen.

So, Lilacia Park was launched with much fanfare. Its fame was enhanced in succeeding years, and nearly every home in Lombard featured old lilacs or new ones as cuttings became available from the propagation area set aside at the park. I had a part in the 1934 pageant, which was written and directed by our neighbor, Katharine Reynolds. Some of my friends and I were assigned to direct particular segments of this large affair, which included whole families - dads, mothers, and children - since the setting was a seventeenth century Village Green in England. It was great fun but hard work as well. After the script was finished, early in the year before, Mrs. Reynolds began assigning directors for such groups as Lilac Dancing Girls, Highland Dancers, Gypsy Dancers, Clowns, Burger Maids, Flower Lady and Children, Fisher Boys, Chimney Sweeps, Bell Ringers, etc. There were buglers, drummers, choruses and music directors as well. It really was a tremendous undertaking, and most of the casts were townspeople and most strictly volunteers. I drew the Burger Maid group who wouldn't have to do much but circulate around, chastising the children at times, mixing into affairs from time to time, and just being women, colorfully dressed in clothing of the period. They were part of the choruses, also. Most of us made our own costumes, and there was such a flurry of sewing in town that year that you wouldn't believe! I also made an orchid and white striped clown suit for my husband who had been chosen as one of the clowns because he was flexible and could do back flips! We took turns meeting with Mrs. Reynolds, group-by-group most every week that spring to get the whole affair coordinated. We were given synopsis of the story and it ran as follows:

Time: *Seventeenth Century*

Place: *A Village Green in England early on a May morning.*

Action: *Bugles and drums and marching men awakened Merry who live with her grandmother in a wee cottage near Village Green. Merry knows that it is Village Fair Day, but can't understand why soldiers from the barracks are* bringing excitement around the Manor House. She hurries about her work and suddenly groups of bell ringers come to proclaim the arrival of the Prince. That means extra festivities. The running crowd goes to meet him as he rides in on a white horse with Highland Dancers and Gypsy musicians surrounding him. The bold leader of the chimney sweeps begs him for a song. He signals for accompaniment and passes among the crowd singing. The villagers sing and cavort on the Green and the Lilac Girls come running, showering him with Lilac blooms. He takes one and tosses it to Merry, the cottage maid, who catches it. Then he rides away.

Now the Fair is on and the clowns, fisher boys, matrons, maids, and bands of Gypsy dancers and fortunetellers circulate gaily. The Gypsy queen tells Merry's fortune, for the girl has been kind to the woman and to the chimney sweeps.

Suddenly a herald arrives to proclaim that there will be a carnival and that a Queen must be found among the dancers on the Green. One group after another dances but no suitable Queen can be found, so the crowd of merrymakers is sent off to town to search for a Queen.

As the crowd runs off stage, Merry dances with the children, all-unconscious of the watching judges. The Prince returns first after the Queen search, and the Gypsy Queen sidles up to him and suggests that the maid dancing with the children should be chosen. The Prince agrees and the bugler's call announces that a Queen has been chosen. The Lilac Girls kneel with Merry as she receives the blessing of her grandmother. Then all wave to her as the guards carry her off to be robed for her coronation. Meanwhile, the clowns go to their routines and the people dance while the singing mistress leads choruses.

For the Grand Finale buglers announce the procession and the Lilac Girls prepare the stage for the arrival of the Prince and Merry who come riding on. The Lord Mayor *crowned the simple cottage girl, who won the admiration of all for her gentle ways.*

Incidentally, he was the actual mayor of Lombard, Samuel Norton!

Staging was on a grassy rise above the rock wall of the pool and must have been planned that way by Jens Jensen for that purpose. There were paths leading to it from several directions in the rear and they were disguised by the thick fringe of lilac bushes strategically placed so that they were hidden from the wide green sward beyond the pool where the spectators sat on benches borrowed from the school gym. Many stood or sat upon the grass as well. The side entrances were from paths between the heavily plumed bushes, which screened the waiting performers from the audiences.

It all was most effective and I might add that the scent of the flowers was heavenly to say the least. Heavenly, also, to stroll through the park at just about twilight in a good blossoming year when it was still light enough to see all of the color, but when the quiet of dusk was at hand the delightful aroma brought a time of enchantment. I well remember that, although I haven't been back for many years.

In the spring of 1980, Lilacia Park celebrated its fiftieth year and there was much publicity at that time about its beginnings. A pageant is no longer held, but festivities last for two weeks, culminating in a parade. The Queen now is selected by the Camera Club and she and her Court add to the Park's attractiveness. Everyone who can gets into the act now to help with finances. Among them are the Chambers of Commerce, Junior and Senior, VFW, the Women's Club, (which was in existence when I was a girl) and the Junior Women's Club, probably an offspring of our old Lombard Girls Club, the Lions and Lionesses, the Education Association, and others. Some of the funds are raised by the annual Lilac Ball, which is held in the first weekend of blossom time.

The little old Lombard that I knew is now as big as a city with some thirty five thousand or more inhabitants. In fact, the whole suburban area, once charming farm and forest country with lush, rich soil, looks like an extension of the City of Chicago because of super highways, one of which cuts through our old property, paved streets and thousands of houses. It is difficult to distinguish Lombard borders from such towns as Villa Park and Elmhurst to the east, and Glen Ellyn and Wheaton to the west.

Incidentally, I used to ride the five miles to Wheaton High over unpaved St. Charles Road on my bike at times. The old high school was near Wheaton College from which the Reverend Billy Graham and his wife later graduated. In sharing these memories with you, I am reminded that most of the good folks who organized the Lilac League have left us, including my parents, who were the first signatories on the Charter. Even the young Adeline Fleege, the first Lilac Queen, would be nearing seventy, if indeed she still lives. In conjunction with these thoughts I'm often reminded of Lorado Taft's inscription on his famous statues of Fountain of Time, situated on the Midway near the Chicago University, which reads, *"Time flies, you say? Ah, no! Time Stays. We go."*

Thousands of visitors stroll through Lilacia every Spring from most of our states and many foreign countries, stopping to admire and to exclaim over some 1200 bushes with more than 275 varieties of lilacs, brilliantly set off by wide rows of many colors of tulips some 70,000 in all. Just being there is a truly magnificent experience, especially when the air is mild and pervaded with that delightful perfume.

Lilac Time in Lombard by Ralph Chaplin

It is lilac time in Lombard and Mystery unseen
Has changed the brown of yesterday to lavender and green;
There's a robin on a swaying twig, a catbird calling near;

And their chorus makes the heart beat high to know
    that spring is here.
In the house a curtain rustles and a fragrance fills each room
For its May time now in Lombard and the lilacs are in bloom.
    To the east the haze hangs heavy where the city looms afar,
Here are cottage yards and parkways with tulips set in rows,
And the breath of cleansing sweetness that the city never knows.
The city's streets are all awhirl with boredom, bliss and gloom,
But Beauty lives in Lombard where the lilacs are in bloom.
    Some people like the towns in Spain of which the poets sing;
Some say that Rome and Picardy are lovely in spring;
But give me good old Lombard with its hedgerows everywhere
And the plumes of purpled glory thrust into the scented air.
Go! Search the world for wonders in color and perfume,
Then turn your eyes to Lombard where the lilacs are in bloom.

Now, a bit of the history of the lilac though the story of the original planting is unknown. However, records show that Busbecquis, Ambassador to the Turkish Sultan, took some from Constantinople to Vienna in 1554. It is interesting to know that Lilacs were found growing wild in 1828 in Romania and in Bulgaria in 1840. They seem to have grown plentifully in England and France in the 1600s but were known by eight or more common names.

Lilacs were introduced into America in the early colonial Days, but records are not verified. The first authentic records are of plantings in Portsmouth, New Hampshire in 1750 and in 1750 and '51 in Hopkinson, Massachusetts. In a letter written in 1755, John Bartrom, founder of America's First Botanical Garden, complained that lilacs planted by early settlers were all too numerous!

George Washington was a flower lover and imported lilacs and many other plants from Europe. His diaries mention something called laylacks that he transplanted to the shrubbery clusters at the south gate. Jefferson also admired lilacs and had them planted on his estate at Monticello.

As is the case of almost all plants known to people in early times, lilacs supposedly had supernatural powers and were symbols of good luck. One could hang the branches over a doorway and prevent misfortune. The common name for the plant in Germany is hollunder, and is named for the Goddess Holla, who was a legendary protector of the household. In England the lilac is sometimes called the pipe tree because the Turkish often made fine pipes of the wood. Another interesting fact is that a medicinal substance, seringin, contained in lilacs is thought to be of value by Romanians in treatment of stomachache and paralysis in humans, as well as for colic in animals. Lilacs are extremely hardy and may be grown in all sections where apples grow successfully - as far north as Alaska, and in all parts of the U.S. except the Deep South.

ANCESTRAL GHOSTS

These ghosts do cast shadows for once they were flesh and blood, kicking and squalling as babies, groping through adolescence, finally fully grown and coping with the vicissitudes of life and times.

Through the deep shadows of the past, nearly a century and a half ago, the vision of a small, dark-haired, blue-eyed- thirteen-year-old girl emerges. Her name was Mary Josephine Buckley and her fifteen-year-old brother, John, accompanied her.

The children had embarked on a sailing vessel from Queenstown, Ireland where they had been born, and after several weeks on the ocean, were met in Boston by relatives, one of whom was a Catholic priest, a Father Toomey, an uncle. They remained in Boston for a short while and then were sent on to other relatives in Philadelphia who arranged for their passage to New Orleans to join their widowed mother, Mary Bates Buckley. This probably was in 1854.

Mary Josephine was enrolled in the Ursalene Convent in New Orleans and her brother attended a Christian Brother's school. There must have been some money although their mother did work as a tailoress who sewed the luxurious silk and velvet, lace and beribboned gowns, which were worn by the wealthy of that day. Little Mary Josephine was to become my maternal grandmother.

She lived with us for about fifteen years as I was growing up and I enjoyed listening to her reminiscences of a happy girlhood in an area of what is probably now known as the Old French Quarter of New Orleans. She enjoyed school, liked most of the nuns and had good friends among the girls. She was a good swimmer and told of the segregated beaches with fences between men and women swimmers. She had stories of the ladies who wanted the convent girls to teach them to swim and how the girls would grasp the women by their long hair and tow them as they floated. She mentioned her mother's displeasure at times when she went swimming without permission and the fibs she told when her hair happened to have dried. Then her mother would feel it and discover the salt in it.

Grandma's hair was almost blue black when I knew her; thick and silky, and long enough to be sat upon. It always was her best feature and remained black and shiny until her death at 81. She had excellent teeth as well and kept them all her life. I don't remember that she ever saw a dentist but she was fussy about cleaning them with some sort of powder, charcoal, I believe. She had nice blue eyes, almost sightless when I knew her, because of scarring by measles as a child and cataracts later. Her skin was fair and with few wrinkles.

I was perhaps seven or eight when she came to live with us in St. Louis and she must have been in her sixties. She was quite active then and must have been quite helpful as a sitter and even in the kitchen, for she regularly baked delicious bread and sometimes helped to prepare other meals. I remember that she liked boiled potatoes in their skins and that she always took out one for herself before they were quite done.

She and Mother had great times talking about *"home"* which was Fredericktown, Missouri, where Mother was born and where she lived until age twenty. I took Grandma for granted as part of the family to such an extent that I was in my teens before I became interested in her stories of her own life. Now I wish that I had asked more questions. Then, I have good memories of her as she sat, a tiny thing, size more pronounced because of a spinal curvature, humped over in her rocker with elbows on her knees, and smiling, as she looked inward to her girlhood before the death of her mother on Christmas Day. Grandma was then only sixteen.

I never thought to ask her how she had spent the years afterward until she met Michael Harris and was married. It seems that she had remained in school for a while and must have been active socially for she did mention balls and festivals and she knew and loved the popular songs of the day. They included those of Stephen Foster, Civil War songs, and Irish ballads. In memory I still hear her singing *Camp Town Races* or *The Harp That Once Through Tara's Halls* in a clear, pleasant voice or teasing us children with a rendition of *Old Dan Tucker* who washed his face in a frying pan, combed his hair with a wagon wheel, and died with a toothache in his heel.

She told of trips to Baton Rouge, which she greatly enjoyed and of pretty jewelry she had worn, particularly earrings, for her pierced ears. She no longer had them as an old lady, for she had given them to her daughters who had passed them on or lost them, but she always kept a broom straw in the openings in her ears to preserve them. She loved to describe some of her favorite gowns in her youth such as the buff colored velvet trimmed in brown or one of sky-blue silk.

Her descriptions of her beloved New Orleans in the late '50s were so vivid that when Phil and I went there a hundred years later, I felt almost as if I had been there before. She had told of the convent and St. Mary's as well as Jackson Square and the buildings with the beautiful iron grill works on balconies and delightful adjacent courtyards, the wharf, the above-ground burials because of the below sea-level land, Canal Street which she always said was the widest street in the whole world and many other things. We were able to tour two of the Catholic Cemeteries endeavoring to find a tombstone with the name of Mary Bates Buckley but without success.

The Civil War was brewing as Grandma grew up. She had long since lost track of her brother when she lived with us but did mention that he had been a soldier in the Rebel Army. I never thought to ask about her courtship with Michael Harris when I was small, but later, when I would have been interested, she had had a stroke and her memory was somewhat affected.

Somewhere along the line I had heard that story of his running away from home in London, where he had been born. His mother had remarried after the death of his father. The family version is that his folks had been florists to the court of Victoria but whether that meant the Harris's or the family of the stepfather whom Michael disliked, I never heard.

The Edward Joseph Costello family, Des Moines, Iowa, 1910. Back: John, E. J. Costello, Grandma Mary Josephine Harris, Margaret Harris Costello holding daughter, Mildred. (Dead at 15 months) Front: Marguerite, and Evelyn.

He must have been a prankster and somewhat spiteful, too, for it was said that the day he left home he found his stepfather napping on the parlor couch after dinner and rushed into the kitchen where he found a fresh fish. He shoved it into the gaping mouth of the snoring sleeper and left home forever.

He went first to Ireland and may have gone to school there. There isn't a picture of Michael anywhere around and he died when Mother was only six so he has always been just a shadowy image to me. I never learned his occupation in New Orleans when he met and courted Grandma but he was said to be good in mathematics and to enjoy working with figures.

Mary Josephine Buckley and Michael Harris would have been married sometime around 1863 or '64. Their first child, Annie, was born in New Orleans on April 8, 1865. Another daughter, Mary, who died, may have been the first.

The Civil War was ending and a few days after Annie was born, President Lincoln was assassinated on April 14. New Orleans was a wild and scary place when the Reconstruction began, and Grandma told of fearsome days and nights when the former slaves began to assert their rights to freedom. There was much rioting and murder and people stayed behind closed doors although that wasn't always safe either.

I presume that is why the young Harris's elected to move North via the Mississippi River and Grandma often told of that fearsome trip when they pulled along side of a burning boat that threatened to sink theirs. Many passengers jumped into the water, preferring to drown rather than to burn to death. She, herself, could swim, and was panic stricken enough to have jumped but was held back. She never forgot that horrible sight.

I don't know why they chose to go to Missouri, but my guess is that jobs on the new railroads were the motivation. The Iron Mountain was being put through and Grandpa went to work for that railroad, as a quartermaster in charge of buying food and supplies for the crews who were moving along as the tracks were laid. I think that the Harris's moved along, too, even living in the cabooses. Grandma said that often there were times when she went over to Cairo, Illinois, herself, to order supplies when her husband was sent elsewhere. Goods were bought in large amounts such as barrels of flour, crates of vegetables, hundred weight bags of navy beans, etc.

Babies began arriving with some regularity and the Harris's finally settled in Fredericktown, Madison County, Missouri, and a lovely part of the foothills in the Ozarks. There was a son, John, after Annie, followed by Jamie, Will, Margaret, and Joey. A sad family story is that one baby was born during a severe thunderstorm and was struck by lightning that killed it. Only four children lived to become adults and one of these, John, died at nineteen.

One terrible winter when Margaret was six, the year 1887, Grandma lost her husband, baby Jamie, and son, John! A severe epidemic of flu type pneumonia took them all. It is difficult to imagine Grandma's desolation at that time. Margaret, my mother, who was six then, remembered that the family had all been packed to move to Kansas City where Grandpa was to have been ticket agent for the railroad. Now she was a widow in her forties and Mother said that after the funerals she took to wearing mourning and never wore colors other than gray, black or white for the rest of her life. I remember that to be so.

Will Harris.

Margaret Harris at 18 years old. (1898)

She hadn't the courage to unpack her furniture until weeks afterward. Her daughter, Annie, then 21, was married to John Regan. They lived close by and were most comforting and helpful. Now Grandma was left with only two children at home, her ten-year-old son, Will, and Margaret, or Maggie, as she was called.

Grandma's religion was a great source of solace as she was a devout Roman Catholic and the priest and nuns at St. Michael's stood by with great moral support. They all were very fond of her. If there was much of any financial support for her in those days I never heard. However, it wasn't long before a windfall came their way, particularly for little Maggie. The story is quite romantic and it involved sister Annie who was a pretty blond young woman. A young man, good friend of her father, had fallen in love with her as she matured and had her father's permission to court her. But Annie had other ideas and fell in love with young John Regan whom she married.

*Annie Regan, Margaret (Maggie,) John Regan.
Anne in background. (About 1900)*

Her suitor, whose name I should remember but don't, for his picture in an oval frame adorned our walls at home for many years, was deeply hurt and maybe somewhat spiteful. He was very fond of pixie-like little Maggie and made his will in her favor. Fate stepped in and he died suddenly, probably of the pneumonia epidemic that was ravishing the area. Evidently he was without relatives, for Maggie inherited five thousand dollars, a goodly sum in those days.

The money was put in trust, guardians appointed by the court, and the interest paid for her clothing, medical bills, schooling, and general needs until she was eighteen. She was enrolled in St. Michael's school in Fredericktown where she had been born on November 13, 1880. One of the trustees, a Doctor Newberry, was also her medical doctor and she had routine medical and dental checkups twice yearly. As Grandma was unable to do her sewing because of poor eye sight, a local seamstress was hired to make up her clothing four times a year so that she was well turned out for all seasons. Doubtless Grandma received some money for her keep, and, as soon as she was fourteen, Uncle Will went to work in the General Store owned by the Pierces who were pillars of the church and good friends of Grandma's.

The Pierces and their customs and peculiarities made great stories for me to listen in on when Mother and Grandma talked about *"home"* as they went about their chores. There were four of them, Mr. and Mrs. William Pierce, brother Andrew and sister, Miss Lizzie. Wealthy by Fredericktown standards, they lived in a suite in the chief hotel, the Madison House. They usually appeared as a foursome, took their meals together at their reserved table in the dining room, attended church on Sundays en masse and bloomed in their finery in their own pew. All worked in the store much of the time. They were kindly, charitable, and well liked even though considered somewhat eccentric. They were fond of Uncle Will, paid him quite well, and helped him to learn responsibility and to grow up. Incidentally his work with them determined his later life in his own grocery business. He was mischievous, witty, and a lot of fun to have around. His popularity with the customers was assured but he was also kindly and helpful to friends in need and once even took physical care of a man with smallpox when no one else would go near him.

Will was four years older than sister Maggie but he and she looked very much alike with their dark blue eyes and crop of thick black hair. Both were small, and folks said that except for the age difference, they could have been thought to be twins. They resembled their mother.

At this time the Harris's shared a large home next to the convent with a Miss Theresa Tucker, who had her own small apartment. She was the sister of Father Tucker and had been his housekeeper when he was pastor of St. Michael's.

All members of the little Harris family were favorites with the nuns next door, but they especially spoiled little Maggie. They soon learned that she was a splendid little mimic and cast her in school plays almost before she was a class member. We have an old tintype photo of her when she was about nine and dressed in a Japanese kimono, complete with obi and pompadour hairdo. The rose-colored grogram sash was among our things as I grew up and I often wangled it for use around my waist or as a hat ribbon.

Little Maggie carried a tiny parasol and sang: ---

I had a little parasol
Long, long ago.
It was just a Japanesie one
Tied with a bow.
T'was only made of paper though.
Just for pretend
I took it in the rain one day.
That was the end

Later, when she was a mother she taught it to us and we in turn taught it to our children.

Grandma used to take Maggie everywhere she went when she was small. Poor woman had lost so many of her family that she hated to leave out of sight those who were left to her. But Maggie was often bored and wiggly in the stiff old horsehair sofas of the parlors of her days and listening to endless lady talk. She usually managed to worry a tassel off a chair arm without being observed by the hostess as a way of entertaining herself. Once, at home when she couldn't think of anything to do while her mother was outside, she found a pair of scissors and, standing before a mirror, cut off her eyebrows. Her mother thought she looked rather strange but it was some while before she discovered why.

Nine-year-old Maggie in Japanese costume. (1889)

Maggie seems to have had a happy childhood. She was something of a tomboy and could run faster, climb trees better, jump higher than most of her friends. The surprising thing is that she never learned to swim since her mother was a really good swimmer. Always a chubby little person, she remained sturdy until about age 16 when she began to lose weight rapidly. There was concern that she might be ill and she was placed under a doctor's care. Evidently that was a mistaken diagnosis for she soon grew well but remained slender and tiny looking.

The social life of the Harris's was pretty much that of their parish. Grandma made delicious bread and her plump loaves were much sought after at the bazaars. She was a good plain cook but left the desserts to Maggie as she grew older and enjoyed fussing with them.

Maggie was reared in the Victorian stuffiness of the late eighties and nineties and her schooling helped this idea along. Besides very good grounding in the reading, writing, and arithmetic area, young ladies learned china painting, embroidery, beautiful Spenserian hand writing, oil and pastel painting, etiquette, and in short, many superficial attitudes toward living. She was quite good at all of the above and her drawing and painting were a bit above average. We had two examples framed and hanging on our walls at home until the death of my father after which my mother broke up housekeeping. Sister Helen took both pictures, one a large pastoral oil painting and the other a smaller pastel. They had been signed and finished in 1896.

I think Maggie loved the school plays most of all and thoroughly enjoyed the comedy parts in which she usually was cast. She must have played the characters to the hilt and when I visited Fredericktown as a young adult I met many of her old friends and was told that Maggie had quite a following - which folks loved to come and see Maggie *"cut up"*.

She often said that she really wanted to do something useful such as to learn millinery design in order to make commercially the fancy hats, which she and all women wore in those days. There were schools to teach that in St. Louis and some of the girls had attended. But her brother wouldn't allow her to consider working. She had gone up to St. Louis a time or two to spend the summer with the nuns and was excited by the big city.

There are several of Maggie's old school books around and the latest of these is dated 1896 so I assume that that is as far as classes went at St. Michael's. She became 16 that year and considered herself quite a young lady. There had always been gatherings of her friends at parties, picnic, outings at the homes of farm friends and such. She had known her favorite boy friend for much of her life and rather took it for granted that they would marry some day.

His name was James O'Connor and his mother and hers had been cronies for years. He was a couple of years older and had begun -- I saw with their good friend Judge Littleton, and was expected to do well in the future. Maggie's best girl friend was Amy Littleton, daughter of the judge.

Margaret and Amy. (1898)

Amy's family were Protestant and though some parishioners frowned it upon, the girls attended each other's churches on some occasions. They attended separate schools but they did every thing else together, shared confidences, wore each other's clothes, or had identical ones made up and so forth.

Both joined a class in ballroom dancing and learned the waltz and two-step of the day. This was about the year 1900. One day Amy confided to Maggie that she had met a new young man named Edward Costello and he had bought a small weekly newspaper in town. He was interesting, sophisticated, and had traveled a great deal. She was attracted to him and hoped he would come calling but would introduce him to Maggie. She did at the next dance.

E J (upper right) with his writing group. 1900.

Young Costello was of medium height and build with dark curly hair, parted in the center in the style of the day, clean-shaven, and with nice blue eyes. He was twenty-three and had an air of glamour and experience about him as he was a writer and in such an interesting profession. He had been born in Wrightstown, Wisconsin of a Protestant and Republican family, technically a Yankee. He was studious, ambitious, but also romantic. What the girls didn't know was that he had seen Margaret *(as <u>he</u> always called her)* on some sort of float, dressed as a goddess in the recent patriotic parade. He always said afterward that it was then he decided she was the girl he intended to marry. He had learned that she would attend the dance and had come especially to meet her. It was practically love at first sight for both. Fate was about to play a trick on two young people of vastly different backgrounds.

Friendship between the girls cooled and James O'Connor was deeply hurt and angry. He expressed this in no uncertain terms to his rival. When marriage was considered there were other problems as Edward was of another faith. Uncle Will was very much against him. Grandma thought that he was a nice young man but wished he were a Catholic. Maggie was stubborn and in love and this was the first major *"fuss."* Folks took sides and many asked, *"Who is this stranger that he should take away one of our girls."*

Edward had one very important ally in the parish priest, Father Rothensteiner, who was also a literary man and himself, a poet. He published a book, which he entitled, a few years later. He and Ed met on an intellectual level and liked and admired each other. But Father Rothensteiner also had been a very good friend to the Harris family for many years and had Maggie's best interest at heart. He felt that young Ed was a decent and moral person and persuaded the family that the marriage looked like a good one

Meanwhile Edward was trying to build up his newspaper, which I think was called the Tribune. He was in competition with the old and popular Democrat News and truly had his work cut out for him. He decided that a popularity contest among the young women of the community would be a good circulation builder and launched one. In the long run it proved a bonanza for the various church congregations that got into it, and battling-for-a-winner became a hot contest. In short he made enough money to finance a honeymoon.

Maggie began to assemble a trousseau and asked a dear friend, Annie Boos, who had trained in St. Louis and was a fine seamstress to make her wedding dress. Ed managed to have himself appointed a Missouri delegate to the Pan American Exposition to be held in Buffalo, New York, in August and the wedding date was set for August 15, 1901.

Father Rothensteiner officiated at the small service, which was held in the priest's home next to St. Michael's. The Harris's gave the wedding breakfast in their nearby home. Sadly, neither Amy Littleton nor James O'Connor attended. The breach between Amy and Maggie was healed some time later when Amy was married to a young architect who took her to live in Baltimore. The happy young couple set out on their wedding trip to Buffalo and Niagara Falls that evening.

Maggie had never traveled farther than DeSoto, where sister Annie and family lived, and had only been to St. Louis a few times, so the long train trip was an adventure in itself. Excitement reached a new high when they arrived in Buffalo and were entertained as newlyweds as well as delegates to the Pan American. There they ran into Ed's old friend and first boss from Ashland, Wisconsin, Joe Mitchell Chappel, who had turned his Ashland paper over to a brother and had gone east to distinguish himself as editor of the National Magazine. He also was an honored guest at the Exposition and he took the young couple under his wing and introduced them to many celebrities. Of course both loved meeting important people and receiving special attention as two attractive and very happy young persons. One of the highlights of the trip was their being invited to attend the banquet of the newly completed Shredded Wheat Plant at Niagara Falls. The guests were served fancy courses in all of which the new product was an ingredient. The menu was kept all of these years and is still around.

As seemed to be the case all of his life, important news had a way of breaking when Costello was around. The young couple was still honeymooning in the area when a man with a bandaged hand who was in line to shake hands with him assassinated President William McKinley. This happened in the Hall of Music as delegates and other officials surrounded him. Ironically, Abraham Lincoln's son Robert Todd Lincoln was among them. So young Ed was in close proximity to one of the notable events of his time, perfect for a young journalist, and he sent off a sad scoop to his little paper back home.

Edward J. Costello and Margaret Harris prior to marriage. (1901)

The young couple was having such a fine time that they overstayed their vacation by a week. Playtime was over for them and real life loomed on the horizon.

Our branch of the Costello family came from Western Ireland in the person of my great grandfather, Patrick Costello, who was a blacksmith. He settled in Hartford, Connecticut, long enough to meet and marry an Irish girl, Mary Hogan, and they became the parents of my grandfather, John, who was born there in 1852.

I never thought much about the occupation of this ancestor until my visit in Ireland a couple of years ago when I learned that the blacksmiths there for a thousand years had been highly respected and often regarded in the manner of judges and poets.

The forges were situated beside main roads, preferably at cross roads where there was a creek with running water nearby. Travelers were eager to stop there, if not to have work done, to refresh themselves and to chat with others, to gather news, or just to fraternize as at a men's club. Women generally stayed away. Often the smith was a mentor as he had access to all sorts of knowledge, but he was busy and versatile as well, for he made a great many important items of the day. Some of these were spades, forks, plough irons, shovels, axes, gates, etc. For the housewives he made, besides cooking utensils such as pots and griddles, candlesticks, knives and forks, scissors, needles and pins, and scores of other necessities. I read that the blacksmith of a century ago could make at least a hundred items and I like to think that since he lived there more than a hundred years ago, he could do that also.

Mary and Patrick had a second son in Connecticut and within a year of his birth, set out westward to the then new state of Wisconsin. They settled in Wrightstown in the Fox River Valley and were living there when the Civil War broke out. Patrick served for the duration, probably as a blacksmith, in the famous Wisconsin Iron Brigade.

He came through the war safely but died in 1868 while crossing a bridge over the river at Wrightstown when it was rammed by a boat and collapsed into the water. There was long litigation but no settlement. His wife, Mary, died five years later in 1873.

Their oldest son, John, my grandfather, then became the head of the family, which consisted of two brothers and three sisters. He tried to carry on as a blacksmith at age 21, but evidently the business was no longer profitable. Soon, too, a brother and sister found mates and the family was breaking up. He found employment, as a machinist with a lumber company and over the years became a very good one with the eventual title of Master Mechanic.

John Costello was a man of medium height but looked shorter because of a limp caused by a poorly set ankle when he was young. He was of slender build and had dark, curly hair and flashing, dark brown eyes and I thought he looked as Spanish as his name sounded. While there I learned that Ireland had had considerable trade with Spain over the centuries and that there are many Spanish names among the natives such as De Valera and Oberon for example, so there must have been a strain of Spanish blood.

John and Eveline Wescott Costello

In 1876 John married eighteen-year-old Eveline Julia Wescott. Her family had moved from the East to a Wisconsin farm in the 1850s. Their family background was Scotch and Pennsylvania Dutch. Her mother, whose maiden name was Ellen White, had migrated from the East as the wife of Edward Brace and after his death had married Artimus Wescott, a photographer. Eveline was born of this union in 1858. I think the town was Sheboygan.

Grandparents, John and Eveline Costello.

My father, Edward, was the first child of this marriage, born April first, 1877 in Wrightstown. John Artimus, called Art, followed and then Maude. A number of years later little sister Margy was born, but she died at age eleven.

For many years the family lived in a rambling house

on the bluff on the north side of the Fox River known as the Stovekin House. Some of Father's happiest childhood memories are centered in that area. The bluff sloped down to a ravine where hickory trees abounded and at the foot of the ravine, near the water's edge, was a tiny shack, which housed a skiff in which the father daily rowed across the river to work. He often spoke with nostalgia of growing up in that wild and beautiful, heavily wooded area near Kaukana where he first attended a one-room school. There was a path along the river's edge, which he fancied to have been worn by Indian and explorer's feet and on which he often trod with his mother while she told stories of the history of that very place.

She told him about explorers Radison and DeGroselliers who, in 1658 and '59, pulled up the Fox River in birch bark canoes, past these bluffs, on their way to Lake Winnibago and out again to Oshkosh and what is now Portage, Wisconsin. She related how they had carried their canoes fifty miles across marshy strips of land to launch them again in the Wisconsin. She had many other tales he said and it may have been the way she told them and her interpretations that began the shaping of her young son's mind.

She had spent her girlhood years on a farm in an area in which Indians still lived. They were friendly, but just in case, she had been taught to use a gun. She said that often one would look up at a window and see a face pressed against the pane. The Indians would be hungry and, of course, they were given food. She rode a horse well and was versed in all sorts of household chores such as sewing and cooking, was religious and a staunch Presbyterian. She loved to read and often played the organ while family and friends gathered around to sing hymns and other songs. She was a strong mother figure,

I never had the privilege of knowing this grandmother very well, for she always lived far from us except for a time or two. She and Grandpa lived next to us in Oklahoma for a year but I was too small to remember much except that one day she took me into her room and kept me, entertaining me for hours while she sewed a lovely new outfit for me to surprise my parents. They always said that I was her favorite.

Grandma was considered a *"fine figure of a woman"* in the parlance of her day. Fairly tall for her time at about five-six, she was buxom and tightly corseted. She had brown eyes and thick hair which she said had turned white during her twenties, but which she discretely colored a deep auburn until she felt it was time to have it turn, rather daring in her day. She was a strong, intelligent woman who was much opposed to alcohol in any form and was a member of the Woman's Christian Temperance Union. Her sons never drank liquor and that alone set my father apart as a journalist.

Grandma was affectionate with her children but the others always teased that Eddie was her favorite. I know that he adored her. He had been a sickly child, born when she was only nineteen, and I gather there were problems with nourishment and possibly allergies. He missed school frequently as he often had colds or grippe as flu was called in his day. His mother would teach him and read to him until he could do it himself at which time he became an avid reader. He loved stories of Greece and Rome, mythology, poetry and Shakespeare. He got his first big volume of the plays when he was twelve or thirteen and read them all. We had that huge book in our home library during my childhood. I suspect that he was what we call today a gifted child.

By the time Ed had reached age sixteen the family had moved to Ashland, Wisconsin, probably following the lumber mills for Grandpa's work. He contracted typhoid fever and nearly died. His recuperation was slow and that summer he found a job on a Lake Superior excursion boat selling candies and other snacks. He reacted well to plenty of fresh air, sunshine and leisure and recovered completely. He seldom was ill all of the rest of his life except for occasional colds or flu.

Father's determination to become a writer was fostered when he submitted some notes to the Ashland Daily Press, and it's owner and editor, Joe M. Chapel, wrote him a warm letter of approval and asked for more items. Young Ed was a student at the Ashland Academy at the time but left after a couple of years to begin his *"career"*. He and another student had published the Courier, which was the Academy paper, and now he was to have experience on a real newspaper. True. And now I quote from his own description. *"Duties included sorting type, feeding off the afternoon editions on the big cylinder press, splitting kindling for the Chapel home nearby, getting up early on bitter cold mornings to start the fire under the rusty boiler that steamed up the coughing engine that turned the stuttering shells of the press."* Yet that job remained the big event in his life until, not long afterward, he was moved into the composing room and taught to set type.

E. J. at the "writing shack" Lombard, Illinois 1924.

It was while he was in the composing room that Guy Durham, then City editor, began to pay attention to him and finally suggested that he might like to be a reporter. Would he ever! And so he became one and learned to *"cover"* police news, report divorce cases and other lawsuits at the county courthouse, and to interview prominent citizens in the town as well as important visitors. Joe M. Chapel moved on to the East and turned his paper over to his brother, John. Joe became publisher of The National Magazine in Boston and was on his way to fame.

E. J. in the first Associated press office in De Moines, Iowa. (1912)

Ed J. Costello, as he signed himself in those days, was learning his craft and loving it. Later, and for the rest of his life, he signed just the initials, E. J. Even at the age of 20 he was beginning to feel uncomfortable that there wasn't such a thing as real press freedom. He was naive at first and thought the plain truth about everything would be sufficient. But, as he always said, he saw too much and asked too many questions, and therefore, fell too easily into editorializing. He learned the hard way that if he wanted to keep his job as an editor he wasn't free to criticize, even justly.

He wrote an editorial on the wasteful methods of the lumber barons in the north woods because he lived in that part of the lumber country. What he hadn't considered was that the Ingram Lumber Company employed most of the townsmen, and although he was careful not to mention the name, he was called on the carpet by the owner and told to go slow in such matters. He learned that, stories were expected to be slanted toward the dictates of the local politicians and advertisers.

*Back row: Gene Kelly and cousin, E. J. Costello.
Front row: Margaret's daughter, Helen, Margaret (Maggie) and Grandfather John Costello. (About 1916)*

Young Ed became imbued with the desire to own his own paper and to try for the freedom of expression. He must have shown considerable ability for the owner of the Iron River Pioneer in a town some thirty miles away went into politics and asked Costello to become editor with a chance to buy the publication. He jumped at it and with the backing of his father he was able to get a loan for five hundred dollars. As he wrote somewhere, *"In those days it did not require a pot of gold to get into the publishing business. Anyone with a shirttail full of type could set himself up as an editor and they were doing it throughout Wisconsin, and east, west, north, and south throughout the nation."*

At any rate, with the money in his pocket, he took the train, and feeling his oats, very grandly stopped at the hotel in Iron River. Filled as we are with the wisdom gleaned from movies and stories over many years, we can guess what happened and it did. Greenhorn that he was, he was enticed into a poker game by some innocent-looking travelers, and feeling his great luck would hold, and that he might double his money and pay off his debt, he was fleeced of the entire amount. That ended that venture and poker playing for the rest of his life.

Then began the roaming of the young journalist through the South. He always was lucky at finding employment on newspapers of all sorts, and in many towns. He worked in Cincinnati, Memphis, Shreveport, Hattiesburg, Mississippi, Jacksonville, Florida, and other places. In Florida he had half a notion to set out to *"to cover"* the Boer War and flipped a coin to determine whether or not he should, the toss proved negative, and he landed in Fredericktown, Missouri, where Fate snagged him.

HAPPINESS IS?

Random House college dictionary says that happiness is (1) the quality or state of being happy (2) good fortune, pleasure or gladness (3) aptness or felicity of expression. Synonyms - beatitude, blessedness, contentedness. Bliss, contentment, felicity - unalloyed happiness or supreme delight such as the bliss of a happy companionship. Contentment is a peaceful kind of happiness in which one rests without desires even though every wish may not have been gratified. Felicity is a normal word for happiness of an especially intense kind. So much for the dictionary. Now to attempt to interpret.

*Evelyn and Elsie sitting on suitcases.
Packed up and ready to go. (1914)*

Since happiness is a very personal expression, often qualified by, *"Yes, maybe for you"*, I can only draw from my own experiences, emotions, observations and memories. I have lived a long life and tend to picture the past as if it had been woven into a tapestry, broad and colorful, and with silken threads of many shades and patterns. There are designs in blues, greens, reds, orange, brown, purple and black. But nearly all are interspersed with gold ones and they stand for periods or flashes of happiness and they are a multitude. Some are in great patches, and others tiny like myriad stars that twinkle in the darkness. There is a strong strand of life and continuity.

One twinkling gold strand flashes and memory projects a little girl of five running with arms outstretched before a brisk Oklahoma wind with the certainty she could fly when a sudden gust lifted her off the ground. I still recall that wonderful feeling of glee and often have tried to renew it, but without success.

Another happy memory comes into focus. We traveled a great deal when I was a child and I, for one, loved it. My younger sister and I had a favorite game that we called *"Packing up."* and we'd find a suitcase into which we carefully packed our favorite toys and books and imagine a train trip to some distant place, sleeping together in a cozy berth, and awakening during the night to hear the steady rumble and clickety-click of wheels on tracks, the watery sound of bells as we approached crossings, the eerie night whistles, and dreaming of the mysteries of the city ahead. This was an educational game as well for we learned to look up cities on the map, to ask about those places, and later, to read about them. And we grew up to be most happy travelers who enjoyed the going and the coming as well as arriving.

Happiness for me always was finding a book under my Christmas stocking, and upon a quick check, noting that my sister got one also so I could look forward to reading two books.

There are degrees of happiness which can be a private matter such as the day the mortgage is paid off, winning at bridge when one trounces a snooty partner, having a new recipe turn out well, getting delivery on a new car, or it can be intense in the laughter after a period of tension. Happiness is widespread in this area when the Broncos win. Happiness is the warm touch of a puppy to a child or jumping into a pile of freshly raked autumn leaves or the aroma of baking bread in the house when he arrives home from school. Happiness must have reached a zenith for Father Jenco when he was released from captivity after many months of suffering, or for Nicholas Daniloff when he knew he was free. That spread a degree of happiness to us all.

Evelyn and younger brother, John. Lombard, Illinois.

But to return to memories, another scene emerges. It

was Sunday morning and nine-year-old, I, was sitting in a pew in St. Ambrose Cathedral in Des Moines with my mother and sister. The well-trained choir was singing and I was listening without paying particular attention until the sweetest, loveliest soprano voice began the Bach-Gounod, Ave Maria. As the organ chords richened and the voice rose ever higher to a thrilling climax, I was ecstatic. I felt more religious and spiritual in that moment than I ever have since. It is difficult to describe that emotion which occurs in a muted fashion every time I hear a beautiful rendition of that hymn. Was that beatitude?

Memory shines on another golden thread. We were still in Des Moines and had lived there long enough to make friends of neighbors and schoolmates. I was to have my very first birthday party ever, and it was planned for our newly-landscaped front lawn. All arrangements had been made for games and refreshments and Mother had taken me downtown to Yonkers to choose my first party dress so that I looked forward with great excitement to that eleventh birthday. Alas, I awoke early on that June 23rd morning and it was raining. Rain came down steadily for several hours and I really prayed for it to stop. *"Oh, please, God, make it stop!"* At eleven o'clock the clouds began to move out and patches of blue appeared in the sky. Before long the sun broke through and the grass began to dry so that by two o'clock when the party was to begin, all was beautiful. The dressed-up young friends began to assemble, bringing small gifts such as fancy cups and saucers, decorated plates, some books, etc. Some of the mothers came to help my mother serve and to visit, and my party turned into an unforgettable success! Pure joy!

Happiness Is?

Evelyn 2nd from left with three friends.

There were a great many happy memories when I was twelve or thirteen. This one in particular stems from our first summer in Chicago, shortly after our arrival. We lived very close to huge and beautiful Jackson Park, which borders on Lake Michigan. It was before six o'clock one balmy summer morning when my father came into our bedroom and gently awoke my sister and me with the words, *"Let's go swimming."*

He was a journalist and had just arrived home from a night assignment. Delighted, we hurried into our swimsuits, the modest-skirted kind we wore in those days, and all set out for the walk across the park in the early-morning stillness. Our destination was the old German Building, left from the turn of the century World's Fair. It then housed bathing facilities where a locker, cotton swimsuit and towel could be rented for ten cents.

It was a lovely walk along the tree-lined paths, which followed the lagoon past the Wooded Island, also left from the Fair. We could see the three Japanese Houses, and Father told us the stories of these and of all of the other places as we walked along, and we felt a cozy closeness to him. He pointed out birds, all sorts of trees, gorgeous flower gardens, all in the early sun which was still casting rising rays over the great lake. We found that only a few people had preceded us when we arrived at the beach, and in no time we stepped into the gently lapping water, shivering slightly. That didn't last long, for soon we were swimming vigorously. Of course we were reluctant to leave when Father was ready to go, but we had an interesting walk back by another route, suits drying upon us. Mother and the smaller children were up when we reached home and a hearty breakfast awaited us. Father went to bed afterward, but our day had begun, a most happy start.

I have another memory from those days in that area, a great one. Our apartment was just across the street from then new and splendid Hyde Park High School that I attended as a sophomore. There were about five thousand students in that block-long magnificent building, with separate gyms as well as swimming pools for boys and girls, a very large auditorium for assemblies and theatrical performances. All classes were going full-blast that pleasant November day when at precisely eleven o'clock whistles began to blow and church bells-to ring, and all of the school doors opened upon the streets. Students and teachers flowed out like a mighty avalanche, crying, laughing, shouting and embracing each other, for it was November 11, 1918, and the Armistice of World War I had just been signed. All of Chicago went crazy that day, streets were jammed, bands materialized, strangers embraced and kissed each other. It was madness, but also sheer joy!

Annitah Yaiser *Evelyn Costello*

It was in those years that I met my friend, Annitah, with whom I've had such happy recent trips to Europe and later to Ireland. She is my age, and we have a lifetime of joyous occasions to recall. I wrote to her to tell her of my efforts to write an essay on happiness and asked for her contribution. She answered that for her, happiness had always been dependent on people she loved and that she was truly happy when she basked in their approval of something she had done.

Happiness for me was a time as a teenager in Lombard, Illinois, when our particular high school crowd would gather for parties at each others' homes and enjoy playing card games such as Five Hundred, with small prizes for the winner, eating the goodies prepared by our mothers, dancing to very good jazz records, or just adventuring as we did one brilliantly moonlit summer's night after one such party.

Evelyn with crowd of Hyde Park High School friends.

Someone suggested that as it was nearly midnight, we roam up unpaved St. Charles Road and visit the small cemetery, which was on the way to the next town, Glen Ellyn. We decided that would be challenging and set out laughing and joking as we rambled along in those days of almost no traffic. Eventually we arrived, and one of the boys opened the creaking iron gate. Some of the braver ones went inside at once and soon the timid ones, myself among those, followed. The tombstones gleamed white and eerie in the moonlight and suddenly there was a scream as a ghostly figure rose slowly behind one of the gravestones! We all raced back toward the road and were well along towards home, not so jolly and speculating on what had happened, when we were joined by one of the boys, who hadn't been missed. He was jubilant and explained that he had hurried on ahead, hidden by trees and bushes at roadside, removed his jacket, and exposed his white shirt, which is what we saw materializing behind the grave. We created our own fun in those days and hadn't the pathetic need of today's youngsters for an artificial high.

Evelyn showing dancer flexibility

Happiness of a more mature sort began to weave its golden thread into my pattern of living when I was around the age of twenty. My father had converted a small outbuilding into a room some distance from the house and named it The Writing Shack. This was his way of getting away from the noise of his children when he had writing to do at home. It was a cozy little place with his desk and typewriter, some bookcases, and a couple of easy chairs. I was always welcome out there for I was interested in writing and he thought I was a natural and taught me a great deal on the subject. I had never gone out to work except for a few weeks of summer jobs at the Federated Press mailing table or helping with proofreading.

I loved to spend time out there when he was away, and would do the homework he had assigned or just take off on my own ideas. One mild winter's day a close neighbor and good family friend stopped me outside and teased me about being lazy. He said he had a job for me, as one of the office girls had left. He was a superintendent at a metal advertising concern in Maywood, about ten miles east of us and reached by commuter trains on the Northwestern. Since I never had any money, I decided to accept.

Evelyn, Lorraine, Marguerite.

I was given a desk in a large office with about twenty other workers. The job was as a billing clerk, and I was pretty green on that subject, to say the least!!! However, it wasn't long before I realized that he also had another motive for hiring me. Shonk Works had an insurance association which also was part social and they put on shows a couple of times during the year, using as many of the employees as

Happiness Is?

wished to participate. An old English Musical Hall actor and his wife, both delightful and talented people directed them. My neighbor knew I had been taking dancing lessons and he thought I would be a good prospect for the shows.

Deciding that would be fun, I picked six of the most likely office girls and taught them a snappy little number called The Jumping Jack's Jubilee. We set about making our costumes, something like romper suits in matching gingham, red and white checked. The company carpenter shop made life-sized boxes with the backs open so we could hop out quickly when the curtain opened as the music started. We worked hard and Director Tommy Carroll and his wife were pleased.

There were several other acts, and rehearsals were great fun. We girls helped with makeup for the fellows, and I had a chance to *"do"* Philip Rucker, who had a comedy part in a sketch and was practically the hit of the show. He also could play the piano after rehearsals so that we all could gather about to sing or to dance. Since I lived in Lombard, which was ten miles west of Maywood, and he lived in Chicago, ten miles east, he and I stayed after work on rehearsal nights and ate supper at a small Greek restaurant near the train station. That is how we became acquainted. There was no romance then, just fun and enjoyment in each other's company. We were in three shows together before romance began to develop. I was twenty-one, and marriage certainly was not on my mind, as I thought I had so much to accomplish to bring my great dreams to fulfillment.

Destiny decided otherwise. There was the time I invited my best girl friend from the office and her beau to come to my home for dinner. To balance things, I asked Phil to come along. He had driven his new car, a Durant, with side curtains, to work so we all set out in it for Lombard. It turned out that that night we had a fierce rainstorm and could hardly see the road. Some parts of the highway were under construction and we slithered about in the mud. It was an ordeal but somehow we reached home. Mother had prepared a lovely dinner, which we all enjoyed, but the rain persisted and it was still quite early when the folks decided to get started on the twenty miles back to the city. I took them out to the car one by one under a big umbrella. Phil was last, and just before he jumped into the driver's seat he turned and planted a quick kiss on my cheek. I really was startled and embarrassed, but pleased as well. However, I couldn't even cherish that kiss for raindrops had washed it away. Bliss and unalloyed happiness often come with first love.

Selected girls for Shonk Works Jumping Jack's Jubilee. Evelyn - extreme right. (1922)

A period of true happiness began with my marriage a year later, weaving the gold threads in a broad pattern, diminishing at times during the years in favor of darker and sadder colors, but always threading throughout until his sudden and totally unexpected death nearly fifty years later. In retrospect, I can find the gold thread even there, for he had had a satisfactory retirement, was 76, and didn't have to suffer any pain or long debilitating illness.

Shonk Works employees in soldier's costumes for the Insurance Association Show. Phil - back row, third from left. Evelyn - first row, third from right.
Evelyn Costello - Choreographer and chorus leader.

No happiness can be greater than that of the young mother, holding the infant that she has just brought into the world in that first tender embrace as she lovingly checks his tiny fingers and toes to confirm his perfection. She remembers her talks to the tiny miracle as she carried him in her body all of those months, for she believed in prenatal influence. She tried to keep her mind uplifted and read beautiful poetry aloud and listened to great music with much pleasure. I must confess that I did those things, and still believe. My two sons are in architecture and music. I must share a day of happiness I had recently upon receiving a thank-you note from one of my California granddaughters for a birthday gift. She finished with, *"And I'll always love you, Grandma, for having brought my father into the world. It would not be so bright a place without him, and his ever-evolving point of view keeps me inspired."*

Close-up of Phil Rucker in make-up for Shonk Works show.

Evelyn as chorus choreographer and leader. (1922)

Happiness Is?

Dave (2) & Doug (6) (1934) • Doug (48) & Dave (44) (1978)

More recent periods of happiness for me have included a trip with dear and knowledgeable friends as we walked in the mountains, observing and identifying moraine flowers and plants up near Pass Lake.

Happiness, too, was a late September trip, again to the mountains, to enjoy the splendor of the aspens, truly spectacular this year. We cruised slowly among the streets of Silver Plume and had the excitement of seeing the colorfully trimmed small houses literally wrapped in golden leaves.

In a recent interview on the Sunday Morning Kuralt Show, Beverly Sills asked Italian director Franco Zefferelli what happiness meant to him. He answered that happiness for him was finding a path through all of the elements of life to contentment. Happiness also was his belief in God.

Lately I have enjoyed reading the book *Courage of*

Conviction by Philip Berman, and have made a note of this quote from an article by Colin Wilson in his contribution to the collection. *"Happinesses from peak experiences are hardly noticed at the time for we take happiness for granted, but as soon as they are recalled they begin happening all over again."* This has been my experience as I recalled some of the golden threads in my tapestry of life. One might say I have been basking in the afterglow of memory so this qualifies as *Happiness Is* rather than happiness *was*.

Confucius said that you cannot pour the perfume of happiness on someone else without spilling some on yourself. I hope I have done a bit of that and I certainly realize that for me, happiness is that I have finished reading this.

Evelyn at home. (1979)

IRELAND TRIP

Perhaps I should give you a bit of background on the friends with whom I took the trip to Ireland in the summer in 1981. Annitah Gorman is my oldest friend as we met in grammar school in Chicago when I was the new girl in seventh grade. Once again I was changing schools because the Associated Press had transferred my father who was a journalist, to that area. Annitah was the one who immediately took me under her wing and introduced me around to her friends.

Annitah Gorman and Evelyn Rucker

She loved to draw and paint and eventually I spent much time after school at her home, sitting across the kitchen table from her as we did homework, sketched or just chatted. I liked her mother too, and often she would serve us slices of cake or other goodies fresh from the oven. Also there were times when she took us down to the Art Institute or to Orchestra Hall or other interesting places. Annitah and I began a lasting friendship, even though my family finally moved to Lombard, Illinois, a Chicago suburb.

Our marriage separated us but we kept in touch by phone calls and visits and even letters. Her only child, Belle was born in the same year as my son David. Both of us had long lasting and happy marriages. I became widowed first. Meanwhile, Belle had grown up and graduated from Northwestern, studied painting at the Art Institute, and received a Masters in Latin and Greek at Chicago University. She married a Physicist who now is a professor at Wisconsin University and she teaches Latin and Greek at a Madison high school.

Annitah and Belle.

Annitah, Eva, Belle.

I had a wonderful trip to Europe a few summers ago with Annitah and Belle so when the invitation came to accompany them for three weeks on a painting and photographing jaunt to Ireland I was delighted. These women do their homework before a trip and know what they want to see and the history of the area. They move about at a leisurely pace driving a rented car, and stopping just any place that appeals to them. They had been over the Eastern part of Ireland and to the north on a previous trip so now would concentrate on the other side.

We took an Aer Lingus tourist flight from Chicago on May 31st, 1981 after a long delay because of a torrential rain. As I want to take you all along on this trip, and since this is St. Patrick's Day, we'll learn something about him during our seven-hour night flight.

St. Patrick was the apostle and patron saint of Ireland. He was born in 373 AD in what is now Dumbarton, England, the son of Roman official, Capernius. As a boy he was captured in a Pictish raid and sold as a slave in Ireland. He escaped to Gaul around 395 A D where he studied under St. Martin of Tours. While there he claimed to have had a supernatural call to preach. In 432 he landed at Wicklow, Ireland, bringing the Latin language and the skill of writing. At first he met with strong opposition but was able, eventually, to convert the chiefs and later the people of Ulster. He founded many churches, including the Cathedral at Armagh where he is said to have died in 464 at the age of 91. However, other areas claim his place of death and burial as he founded churches throughout Ireland. There are many legends, among which is the one that he rid Ireland of vermin as well as of snakes. It is said that he used the Shamrock to illustrate the Trinity to the heathen priests, more about St. Patrick later. We have arrived at Shannon Airport and picked up the little rented car, a British Ford.

We set out toward the northwest for the town of Ennis where we found what seemed to be the main business street and shopped for some groceries to carry along. The street was lined with small shops, a few with earthen floors, and we went into a butcher shop with meats hanging in windows as we remembered once happened back home in the early days. Although it was raining lightly, Belle pulled out her camera and tried for a few pictures. One was of a small boy trying to sell his pony at what seemed an outdoor market.

Apartments and shops facing the harbor.

It was well after noon and we decided to head for Malby and the Spanish Point area. On the way we had our first good look at the green of Ireland washed and enhanced by the showers. We found an attractive place to stay at St. Brendon's that was the home of a Mrs. Sexton who chatted pleasantly and told us that she was to serve as an usher in costume at the performance of South Pacific that her church was giving that night. She suggested that we might like to attend and assured us that it would be quite professional as they had excellent singers and had hired an expensive director. Then she showed us to our rooms and took the time to trundle in a serving of tea and scones that were most welcome. We turned in early and hardly needed the rhythmic lulling of the waves to sleep soundly that night after having little rest on the long plane flight.

My duty was to keep the journal while they painted or

took photos and the three weeks netted some fifty pages typewritten. I have condensed them to about ten but will give the diary of the first full day so that you'll have an idea of the pace.

Sunday, May 31, 1981

We were happy to see sunshine when we awoke and were well rested and alert when Mrs. Sexton knocked. We followed her into the bright dining room when three small tables were set with white linen and pretty china and silver. Four Americans who were visiting relatives in the vicinity occupied two. They were two couples and we chatted pleasantly as we ate. Since this was our first meal at a B and B stop we were curious about what foods would be provided. We enjoyed a hearty meal of Canadian bacon, sausages, scrambled eggs, Irish soda bread and marmalade. We could have had a cereal also if we had wished. Before setting out on the day's adventures we asked to have our thermos bottles filled with hot water for tea or coffee later.

Now we are headed north along the coast road that practically hugs the Atlantic toward the Cliffs of Mohr. The pale blue sky is somewhat cloudy and we can hear the waves crashing in as we view the endless sea. We'll be traveling along this craggy route much of the day, stopping often for good picture angles. At the moment I am sitting in the car to write while Annitah and Belle are scouting for places to photograph or to paint. We have parked beside a memorial in bronze which commemorates the gallant stand made by the officers and men of the Mid Clare Brigade against the forces of the British in September, 1920 and the conflicts of 1917 and 23. It is the statue of a soldier and is backed by a very high hill.

We have reached the magnificent Cliffs of Mohr. Annitah is uncomfortable at heights so we have left her below at a good vantage point while Belle and I scrambled up the steep, grassy slopes of one of the Cliffs. Now, while Belle checks for good angles, often hanging over a ledge on her belly as she aims for something below, I am perched upon a huge stone absorbing into my soul some of the most fantastic scenery of my life! The strong waves explode into foam at the bases of the Cliffs, which stand as sentinels at inlets as far as I can see.

Cliffs of Mohr.

The undulating Atlantic is deepest blue nearby but faces gradually to lighter shades as it approaches the horizon and dissolves into sky. The air is delightful to breathe and the winds are gently caressing. Far below the area is coming alive with hikers and picnickers on Sunday holiday and I can see a couple of vans dispensing items while a small group of people begins a climb up another of the cliffs in the distance.

When Belle had finished we moved slowly down the incline to join her mother and when we had nearly reached the bottom, all three enjoyed the firm right arm of a young Irishman for the final leap from a high stone! Everything in this lovely country is of interest to all of us. For instance the road signs in Gaelic with English translations printed below the narrow but good roads that twist and turn weirdly, the landscape, usually hilly, often mountainous, divided into small parcels by ancient rock walls, stones perfectly cut and laid, miles and miles of them, the green pastures, the sheep, with long-hairs with black faces and hooves marked with splashes of bright paint to indicate ownership and often resting practically on the highways, cows nonchalantly making their way, more or less together, along the roads to pastures, dogs often working the cows, but almost as often lying down anywhere they wished even if that is in the middle of the road! Most seemed gentle and loved and no one bothered to chase them!

Sheep by the road.

Once we stopped to investigate the ruin of an old stone house, set in an overgrown lot. The center room was very large with a huge fireplace at one end and smaller room on each side. There was a stone shed attached to one of those. The roof had fallen in at the back but toward the front and near the chimney the old thatch had sprung to life and was filled with wild grasses, some even in bloom.

We saw a number of such houses as we traveled about, but at times we noted new houses standing beside the old ones and wondered if possibly some former émigré had returned to claim family property. Belle would have liked to buy one to fix up to live in on future trips to paint. Of course we were out in the country but we saw few people as we moved about. It seemed as if all of this beauty was there for us alone to enjoy!

Annitah and Evelyn seated by a dolman.

We continued along the coast road with the sea always to the left of us as we headed for the barren area near Lisdoonvarna. The place is of interest to geologists as it is floored in large, flat limestone rocks and is sort of a limestone dessert, which is called a karst.

*Irish castle. (Not the McLaughlin Castle of Burren.)
It was after nine when we reached our lodging and Mrs. Sexton was still out doing her usher stint at the church, but her daughter kindly trundled tea and cakes into our room and we thoroughly enjoyed them before turning in.*

Ireland Trip

Wide shales and flagstones are plentiful and streams disappear into potholes. There are underground rivers and caves and many types of flora flourish in cracks and crevices of one sort or another. In prehistoric times this area was well populated and there are remnants of stone forts and Dolmans, ancient burial places made of box-like stone formations, topped with huge, flat boulder roofs. We explored all around them and Belle took pictures.

It was late but still very light when we started back to last night's lodging after making one more stop at a Burren museum where we heard a lecture about the area. This was in Kilfenora.

We have just driven past Spanish point where part of the great Armada was wrecked in a wild storm and where Spanish crewmen, lucky enough to survive, swam ashore. Maybe not so lucky for they were imprisoned by the British and most were later executed. There went my belief in legend that my maiden name, Costello, arrived in Ireland then!

And so the days went by, each as anticipated with eagerness and excitement. We continued northward on the coast roads and on Monday traveled over Devil's Corkscrew Road near Slieve Mountain (love the names) to the great McLaughlin Castle of the Burren. Belle and I climbed the spiral stone stairway to the top of this ruin dating back to the Middle Ages. Originally the structure was L shaped. I pressed against the stonewalls for support and soon dirtied my hands with bird droppings but that was all part of the adventure and we had a marvelous view of the ocean on one side and miles of interesting landscape on the other.

Village across the water.

On the way to Galway we went through a rocky and bleak area and wondered how people survived there but a little further on we came into bog country and saw our first bog cotton. Finally arrived at Kyle Pass and Annitah and Belle began to look for Connemora marble which is green although there is white marble as well. I found a pretty large stone with green on one side and white on the other. Sadly it weighed too much for my baggage.

At Galway we parked beside an inlet on the Bay where several boats were docked. Had a good view of the homes across the water and the gals filmed them. We were near a lot beside a playground where boys were at games as this was a bank holiday. We decided to have lunch there and brought our thermos bottles of hot water to make tea for them and instant coffee for me. We made good sandwiches with brown bread, cheese and tomatoes. We also had apples and crisp cookies along. We always carried a variety of fruits, cakes etc. We always found fantastic places to stop for lunches. If there was a town nearby we would buy tea in mid afternoon and dinners always were eaten in restaurants after we had stopped at our lodging to wash up.

We continued driving north through Galway to the area of Cong, which has been called one of the greatest places of natural beauty and historical interest in all Ireland. The Celts, almost the first Irish, arrived about 350 BC. Before that strange mystical people, small in stature, and tribal, ruled the country. We visited the famous Abbey where St. Feichen had founded his first monastery in 627 AD. St. Patrick had begun his first mission in Ireland in 432 AD and had established the Christian faith in every part of the country. Students from England and the Continent came to study at monastic schools and there were about three centuries, which were known as the Golden Age. Ireland became known as the island of Saints and Scholars. The Norse invasion brought an end to all of this.

The present Abbey, now a ruin, was begun in the twelfth century and was partially destroyed many times but restored each time. We strolled about in the Cloister garden area and found a path, which led through a thickly wooded plot to the dark river and followed that to the little stone fishing house set out into the water. It was entered from a small footbridge and there was a hole in the floor center of the little building through which the monks could drop a fishing line and wait in comfort for the dinner catch. We felt an eerie and brooding beauty about the whole area that day.

Belle had chosen Achill Island in County Mayo as our north-most goal and we fell in love with it almost at once, although there was rain nearly every day of our stay. Part of our pleasure was the time spent in the home of David Quinn and where we settled down to the comfort of home. They were a retired couple and Mr. Quinn had been the island schoolmaster for fourteen years. Mrs. Quinn invited us to the small dining room and served tea and freshly baked cake as she chatted with us about the island. We learned that Achill was the largest and most westerly of the islands, that there were several complete villages along the coast, that it was famous for it's scenery and that tourists were late this year because of the rains!

We stayed with the Quinn's for four nights, always free to return at any time, even during their absences. One day was spent out in a real gale and our damp clothes had to be placed in a drying room. After changing to dry ones we were invited into the living room where the fireplace glowed with a bright peat fire and Mister Quinn was watching TV.

The program covered the British Sweep Stake races. We watched with him while Mrs. Quinn prepared and brought in some tea and scones. I had a talk with her about the "troubles" in Belfast and she told me that she had lived in that city and that her sister, a nursing nun, had been killed on the street when she and others passed a bombed car nine years ago. She had grown up in Belfast and her best girl friend that lived next door was a Protestant. Catholic herself, she and her friend used to attend each other's church services on special occasions. She felt that the troubles were far more political than religious and wished that Americans would quit sending money to Ireland for she said the funds were wrongly used for ammunition. I asked if she feared returning there and her answer was, no certainly not, that she often visited her folks there.

So the days went at Keel and surroundings, and we had an exciting and rewarding time going over every area. We looked into all of the villages, visited and bought in their gift shops, talked to the proprietors, ate in their restaurants, drank in the beauties of their coastlines, visited their cemeteries and ruins, and dallied on their golden strands as the few beaches in this cliffy country were called.

Strange vertical building. (Once Grace O'Malley's castle?)

Belle was interested in the light under various conditions and we went out every day, even though it rained, and one day we came upon the Grace O'Malley Castle. We plowed through the tall wet turf to reach it and Belle and I climbed the circular tower stairs to the top and looked out at the sea. Grace O'Malley was a pirate queen who lived at the time of Elizabeth the first of Britain. She was fabulously rich and was a heroine to the Irish for she was generous and her exploits were admired. Her rival Queen never defeated her although Elizabeth probably did some pirating on her own. The story goes that Grace had several husbands and that she rid herself of one by pushing him from this tower to his death on the rocks below! This tower provided a marvelous lookout. We could easily imagine the appearance of ships as they sailed in from the horizon. We also looked down at the rocks below and thought of that poor husband!

We were reluctant to leave when the time came, but

headed south along the coast, retracing the route along the highway for a while into Newport, then down to Westport into the Connaught area, through Galway and into County Clare where we took the ferry across the Shannon from Kilrush to Tarbet in Limerick County. There isn't time to recount all of our stops like St. Patrick's Round Tower, which, like others was built as a lookout to alert churchman if intruders appeared on the horizon.

At some point on Bally Keen Road we stopped to see the partially restored church of St. Patrick. We were crossing the churchyard when we noticed a young couple peering into an opening in a building adjacent to the larger one that was roofless. Finally they turned away and the young man said to us. *"There's a pile of bones n there!"* With a touch of horror, we looked into what Belle said was a charnel house, explaining that when old graves were dug up, the bones which hadn't deteriorated were brought up and tossed into a certain room which had been blessed as were the original graves. It seemed irreverent to say the least, actually gruesome to me, that those piles of arms, legs, skulls, pelvic bones and others should lie there exposed to the elements through a doorless opening to await the day of judgment, I supposed.

Another interesting stop in this vicinity was the church at Balleytubber Abbey, a beautiful one that had been restored and in which Mass has been said continuously since 1216 in spite of massive attacks and rebellions. Cather Grovesdearg O'Connor, King of Connaught, started it.

Vegetation seemed to thicken, to change somewhat as we followed the peninsula fingers down to the Southwest tip of County Cork and put up at a small family hotel in the city of Skibbereen, a harbor and fishing town. Now we saw palm trees, azaleas, on great heavily blooming bushes, profuse fuchsias and other tropical plants that attested to the year-around mildness of the climate in this area. We learned that the Spanish had originally brought many of these plants

Ireland Trip

from the Mediterranean, centuries ago.

We stayed in Skibbereen several days, always driving out from it in the mornings and back at night for we were comfortable in the rather shabby little hotel with pleasant people around. It was called Ilen's Guest House and the young schoolgirl daughter who had first shown us our rooms impressed us. She told us that she had been busy studying for exams and that she had to pass ten of them to get her high school diploma! When we took our reluctant leave, Mr. Collins, the proprietor, carried our luggage out, stowed it in the car and bade us God speed.

I should say here that everywhere we went we found the people courteous, a little reserved, but always friendly. The level of education was high and Gaelic is the first language for students with English second.

All students are bilingual which is a wonderful plus. We saw no evidence of poverty, perhaps because we didn't stop at large cities such as Dublin. All of the while my friends were gathering hundreds of slide shots and I was sitting on stumps, rocks, cliffs, in the car, writing pages of notes for my journal and ended up with forty-four pages, typewritten stuff which I have condensed considerably for the present account. The spirit of daily adventure continued to the end.

I'd like to mention one other place, which was a favorite. That was the Dingle Peninsula and the town of the same name. We were on our way there when we had a bit of excitement. We turned off the road to have a view of another Castle and it was raining slightly as we passed the empty gate house but decided to take the long narrow road a half mile or so, only to find the iron castle gate chained.

Belle took a quick turn off the road into the heavy wet turf, expecting to turn around. No such luck! We became bogged down and all three together couldn't budge the little car. There wasn't a soul around and the drizzle continued. Finally Belle started to walk back to the highway and told us to stay in the car.

It was lonely there and rather dark and gloomy under the dripping trees and no soul was in sight. We looked out to one side and saw a slip of water and a couple of empty boats anchored. On the other was the chained gate and we thought that probably it wasn't locked. We could have eaten lunch but weren't hungry as we were concerned about Belle and our predicament.

Slip of water and a couple of empty boats.

Here we were, two old ladies sitting in a car, targets for robbery or worse, for all we possessed was with us in the way of money, passports, luggage, etc. Then we remembered that several times we had heard that the crime rate in Ireland was very low, that there almost never was a robbery, that we had found people most trusting in that some of the store proprietors had allowed us to figure the exchange rate and one even allowed Annitah to tally up the cost of her purchase and to pay with a personal check on her Madison bank! We had been told at several B&Bs to come in at any time whether or not any one was home and one lady even left her key under the doormat for us! Then we began to giggle that we should work out an Agatha Christie plot for a mystery, as this was a perfect setting, but about then Belle came riding up with two men who pushed us out in no time.

The Castle gate wasn't locked so we undid the chain and walked in to stay for quite a while exploring this large ruin which had been most elegant in its day. Also, it had probably given its name to nearby Castletown. We drove along the highway that clings to the cliffy coast and arrived at the town of Dingle near the western tip of the peninsula.

Belle and Annitah had stayed at a farm B&B in the area and we went there to find Mrs. O'Doud, a very pregnant young woman who let us rooms. We were placed into a very nice building near the house proper and hoped to stay for a few days but the next morning we were told that the baby was due and that Mrs. O'Doud was on her way to the hospital, so would have to close the house.

We found another place further out in the country and it was rural indeed but was close to the ocean and my room overlooked the bay. I loved that. We used this place as headquarters and drove out each morning to explore and into Dingle for shopping and great fish dinners at the restaurants.

A time or two there were other boarders for breakfast. One morning when we went down to eat, there were two others at table, a young couple from Berlin, Germany. The young woman told us that she was a social worker back home and she spoke beautiful English almost unaccented. Not so with the young man, pleasant faced and darkly handsome, but who spoke little. Annitah began telling them that she had been gathering seaweed and other plants for her collages when she got home but that she couldn't pack them in her luggage for fear they would be thrown out by customs if they checked. She explained that she would wrap them in some of her clothing and mail them to herself in the States. The young man began to laugh and turned to say to his wife in strongly accented English, *"Soo, ve got mit us a plant smuggler!"* We all had a good laugh

We were staying near Dunquinn and the Blasket Islands were directly across from town. We tried to get over to them but the launch wasn't running on the day we planned to go. Word all over town was that the young man who ran the launch had a brother, ill in a hospital, and all thought that probably he had gone to visit him. We were quite disappointed as the Great Blaskets are very famous and were inhabited until 1954. People had lived on these several islands for centuries as farmers, cattle and sheep raisers, or fishermen.

They handled the little curraghs skillfully and came across to Dunquin on special occasions but were generally clannish and kept very much to themselves. I bought several little books written by natives of the Blaskets and literary talent seems to have flourished there. Some of the white houses can be seen below the mountains but no one really lives there any more except those who keep the summer supplies for the tourist trade.

On our scouting trips we saw such things as beehives, so called because they are constructed with stones corbelled to the top and closed to keep out the rain. They were the dwellings of the ancient inhabitants and were built about three thousand B.C., but some continued in use until the seventeenth century. Those survived the Norse and Norman invasions. One of the most perfectly preserved is the Gallerus Oratory that was a Druid Place of worship.

In one old cemetery we saw an Ogham Stone. Ogham is a very ancient language and is the first known written language in Ireland. The alphabet was derived from a form of Greek in the sixth century B.C. It consists of twenty-six sounds and was originally a sign language used to communicate secretly by the Druids. Cumbersome and not intended to be written, eventually it was, first on wood and then on stone. Three hundred Ogham Stones have survived and half of them are in the Dingle area. The writing is incised on the edges, strokes to the right and left across the trunk line, and they read from the ground upward. Because the stones contain the oldest written language and most of them are located in Dingle, the town may well lay claim to having been the center of learning and culture in pre-historic Ireland.

Well, there is just too much to tell so I'll move on to the next to last day which was in the town of Kilkee, County Clare, where we stayed at a lovely home at which Annitah and Belle had spent time on their last trip. Mrs. Griffin welcomed them as old friends and treated us royally. We set out the following morning to explore the area and had driven only a short distance from the house when we spotted a white hare leaping across the rocky floor below the coast road. The tide was out and a white floor was exactly what the flat rock table resembled. We climbed over the large bumpy boulders on the way down and reached the wide flat ones, barren rock, I guess, below. We could see that some were beautifully wave sculptured and others were slightly hollowed out and water-filled by the retreating tide. Two young women we had noticed before were near the splashing waves on the distant shore and no one else was around. Just walking there seemed to make our feet light and as if we were having a wonderful adventure, strangely exhilarated, rather like children running before the wind! The air was sweet and clean and the Atlantic a deep blue in the morning sun so that just being there and feeling so aware and in tune brought a sense of enchantment. We all felt it.

The gals filmed vegetation in some of the deeper crevices and potholes and we saw limpets and other sea creatures. We spent the whole morning there and saw only one other couple after the two girls left. They were English travelers and they admitted that this wide area had cast a spell over them, too! They mentioned that their home was near Oxford and, since we all had visited there on the last trip, we had a pleasant topic of conversation.

From there we took the road out into the country toward the town of Cross and stopped at a farm gate to eat lunch. We were amused when the cows began to wander over to the gate and finally the whole herd seemed to be waiting. We decided that they were used to coming there when the farmer came in a car to lead them home. When they realized he wasn't coming, they began to move away, all but one stubborn one, which just stayed there looking at us until we left.

Belle shot a picture of her mother and me when we came to a picturesque old ruin near Kilbaha. Soon we were in a lovely little town, Cross, and the only person we saw was a young priest who came dashing out of the Post Office to ask if he could be he helpful. He said he was a native but had been to America which he liked very much and that he would be going back again to Virginia in the summer. He told us about his neighborhood and that he had filmed a story there a couple of years ago. It was Ryan's Daughter. He pointed out one house, which the movie company had used, and Belle took its picture. Then she handed him her camera and he took ours and we took one of him in front of his church. He also mentioned that several movies by American companies had been filmed there besides the oldest that was *The Quiet Man.*

After leaving Father Doody, we drove off to see the Bridges of Ross, remarkable ones made from the cliffs along the coast where the relentless dashing of the waves over the centuries had hewn them.

The day before we left for home we went again to visit the Lakes of Killarney, one of the loveliest areas of all, and hiked again up the incline to the head of the great falls which seem to emerge from an under ground river. They tumble over rocks and vegetation a long way before reaching the stream that takes them to one of the great lakes.

Ireland Trip

We had enjoyed that part of the park on the former visit and this time we decided to see the rest of it by taking the horse-drawn cart through other magnificent areas to the Muck Ross Mansion that had been deeded to the Irish Republic by American owners, if I remember correctly. Our driver was a youngish man who helped us to climb up to the high side seats. We enjoyed talking with him and he was pleasant and informative. The white horse was named Sue and I am sure she could have made the trip without him. He dropped us off at the mansion and we spent considerable time touring this splendid house. It has been brought up to date although it contains much of the original elegant furniture and it has a fine museum on the first floor. We browsed in the formal gardens that are exquisite and perfectly groomed.

Elle, Evelyn and driver.

Friday, June 19, 1981. Rain! Packing was finished last night so I had to haul out the light raincoat and fill the space with a too bulky sweater! We ate a leisurely breakfast and visited with Mrs. Griffith who has been most cordial and invited us to return. We drove through Kilrush and on to the airport where we hoped to check our luggage through. Too early, we left to drive to Bunratty Castle where we had tea before beginning a tour of the estate. It was most interesting, particularly the reconstructed houses of the various classes from the poorest to the rather elegant one of the wealthy farmer. Some even seemed occupied and had peat fires burning in the fireplaces. Also, the scents of baking goodies permeated the atmosphere.

    Afterwards we spent two hours touring the beautiful castle, then headed back to Shannon Airport. Belle turned in the car and then came the long, long wait in the luggage check line! After clearing security there was still time to browse in the duty free shops until finally came the call to board the Aer Lingus flight for home.

THE RALPH CHAPLIN STORY

In line with the theme, American Heritage, this year for the Delphians, I'd like to tell the story of a man who was a neighbor in our little town of Lombard, Illinois when I was young. His name was Ralph Chaplin. He was an artist, poet and writer, a charismatic speaker, a patriot and a rebel.

He came by that naturally as his ancestors must have been rebels as well, at war with their generation as he was with his.

GRANDMOTHER BRADFORD
Wartime photograph of my grandmother, Alma S. Bradford. Memphis, Tennessee.

GRANDFATHER BRADFORD
My grandfather, Arwin A. Bradford, wore Union blue during the War between the States.

Ralph Chaplin's grandparents.

The Chaplin Family had left Rowley, Yorkshire, England in 1638 and settled in New Rowley, Massachusetts. Ralph's mother was a Bradford and they had already been established in Vermont when the Chaplins arrived.

The grandfather of Ralph's dad had fought in the Battle of Saratoga under General Gates in the Revolution. His mother's father, Grandfather Bradford, remained in the army after the Civil War and participated in several Indian campaigns under the regime of General Custer. Ralph's father had been a Drummer's Boy.

Ralph Chaplin's parents. (1885)

The elder Chaplins had traveled by wagon train to Wisconsin after the Civil War and from there to Kansas where they settled in Cloud County. They were quite poor when they arrived but they had a team of horses and a quarter section of rich soil so they didn't feel poor. As Ralph wrote in his 1948 biography, they felled scrub cottonwoods along the banks of the Republican River to build their first

The Ralph Chaplin Story

cabin. There were no crops that first year but they could live on buffalo and antelope meat. Wild ponies roamed the plains and his father roped and tamed some. The government supplied McClellan rifles and ammunition and God supplied the sun and rain. The rest was up to them.

They loved the life, felt secure, and prospered for a number of years. A daughter and two sons had increased the family when the panic of 1886 struck the nation. The father had had an accident while taming a pony and had lost the sight of one eye so was advised that continued work in the glare of the sun on buffalo grass could cost the sight of the other.

After much agonizing the family left for Chicago with a load of cattle for the stockyards, there Ralph was born in 1887. The family was forced to live in a poor section of the big city where the father found work at a railroad-crossing tower. Ralph's sister had remained in Kansas and his brothers soon left home to find work so he was reared much as an only child. His mother was artistic, musical and a reader. They had managed to keep the old organ, which she often played. She saw that Ralph had talents and encouraged him in his drawing. The family became friendly with an elderly man in the neighborhood who owned a bookstore and Ralph was allowed to borrow books so that he learned to read voraciously. In that manner he discovered the great classical authors. After school he often went to the railroad tower to visit with his father and to listen to his tales of the Kansas days and the life, which his father had loved. At home his parents continued their religious ways of morning and evening prayers as well as those at meal times. Theirs was a loving and gentle home.

Ralph was extremely bright and talented but he often found school a bore. His companions came from low income and depressed families. Most such boys at the turn of the century had little to look forward to, as they would be lucky to finish eighth grade. They were anxious to find some sort of work so as to help out at home. Wages were pitifully low and working days usually began at dawn and ended at dark, twelve to fourteen hours in all.

The crowded city's lower classes were beginning to stir and to ask why they had to work so hard to make their employers so rich. Ralph often went to the corner of Sixty-third and Halsted Street to hear speakers urging workers to organize. He was fascinated and began asking questions. It was around that time that his father lost his job at the railroad tower. Ralph was furious that a man's livelihood could be taken away for no fault of his own. Fortunately, his father found work much more to his liking attending the horses of a huge livery stable.

Ralph Chaplin (1909)

Ralph was thirteen at the turn of the century and had already earned a few pennies as a newsboy, often jockeying with others for a favorite corner. Also he had worked at the loading platform of a department store where he used much strength and effort to prove his worth for the five-dollar weekly wage. He was more than pleased when the boss complimented him and gave him a dollar raise but his delight faded when he learned that another boy had been fired so that now the boss was getting the work of two boys for six dollars. He quit. Then, at the next Halsted Street gathering he shyly told a man what had happened. He was pulled to the platform and asked to repeat his story. There was much approval and he felt the exhilaration of speaking publicly. That was prophetic.

One of Ralph's teachers was impressed by his drawings and cartoon's and suggested training. She helped him to get work at an airbrush studio on Michigan Avenue and he found himself in a different world. Here his companions were culture oriented, creative and individually most interesting. He was introduced to symphony concerts at Orchestra Hall and to Chicago's already famous Art Institute where he later took night classes. He heard intellectual arguments and discussions and soon began to participate in them. His reading continued and he discovered the Great Russian writers, Tolstoy and Ivan Turgenev *(after whom he later named his son Ivan)*. He read and admired Jack London also, and later was to illustrate some of his books. Incidentally, Ralph resembled him somewhat physically as both were big and strong and had rugged good looks. Both had similar ideals as well.

Ralph spent a great deal of time educating himself and in realizing his other talents. He discovered his writing ability in both poetry and prose and began to practice. He also discovered lovely Edith Medin who worked at the studio as an airbrush artist and later was to marry her. He took lessons in public speaking as he had an urge to do some of that when he realized the great social injustices in the labor world of 1914.

Class wars of all sorts darkened the map of America. The sweat shops in the East in which the people, children among them, slaved for pittances fourteen and more hours a day so that they seldom saw daylight, were prevalent. In Chicago, Upton Sinclair's book, *The Jungle*, was published and exposed the filthy conditions in the meat packinghouses and the stockyards. The public became so revolted that many people, my parents among them, became vegetarians. Pitiful, horribly unsafe conditions prevailed in the country's mines in West Virginia, Illinois, and the one at Ludlow, Colorado, was a tragic example of the exploitation of human workers. It was owned by John D. Rockefeller and was one of the worst, a true example of industrial serfdom. Schools, churches, stores, housing shacks, even the Post Office, all were on company owned land. Wages were paid in scrip instead of U. S. currency and averaged less than two dollars a day. Just entering the black holes of the mines was a challenge in itself.

Conditions and the time were right and it wasn't too difficult to persuade the miners to organize and protest. The real trouble came when they decided to strike and the state called out the militia when strikebreakers moved in. The horrible massacre of miners, their wives and children is well documented. Women's groups even picketed the Rockefeller offices in New York to no effect.

Ralph considered it patriotic to try something for the majority of workers. He had learned that many of the great fortunes of America were being made in that exploitive manner. Reading some of the revolutionary history of the past inspired him. To him Winwood Reed, *The Martyrdom of Man*, read like fiction and extended his horizons to include the history of the Human Race and its institutions. He constantly sought answers and he found one to the question of why workers meekly seem to accept their lot to make someone else rich. He got an answer from a man on the soapbox at Halsted Street who pointed out that the individual was helpless alone. Workers simply had to group together to help themselves.

Ralph began to lose time from the studio as he was gaining the reputation of a good speaker and was called upon to address large gatherings of miners, railroad, workers and others. Inevitably the unionizing workers invoked the power against themselves of the very money, which the bosses had realized at their expense!

Edith Chaplin (1906)

Whole libraries have been written about the struggles of the Labor Movement in the early part of the century and later Ralph played his part. He began to write articles, which were widely published along with some of his poems and cartoons. He was gaining a reputation and a good following among readers. He also found time at an early age to marry Edith Medin. She was a pretty young woman, bright, sweet and understanding as well as a good commercial artist. Theirs became a most happy and lasting union. She continued to work at the studio but was alone much of the time as her husband traveled often.

Unionism was catching on and eventually tangible results began to emerge in spite of great opposition. Gradually working hours were shortened first to nine hours a day, six days a week. Later came the eight-hour day with five and a half days a week with overtime pay after that. Wages were figured on an hourly basis, still low but somewhat improved. Child labor laws went into effect so that children under fourteen could no longer be exploited.

Woodrow Wilson marching in a Liberty Loan Parade

The Ralph Chaplin Story

The great middle class was beginning to emerge. Battles to achieve this had been horribly cruel at times and many leaders had been imprisoned, some unjustly. Many people striving for the rights supposedly provided by the constitution, especially the one of free speech, had been clubbed to death or put away in some other manner.

Often, the very people who would have benefited greatly by the unions turned against them. In a sense a real war was being waged, a class war.

Now it was 1917 and World War I was looming on the horizon. It had begun in 1914 between European countries ruled by three grandsons of Queen Victoria. They were George the Fifth of England, Kaiser Wilhelm of Germany and Czar Nicholas of Russia. The United States was tottering on the verge of entering the war but the majority of Americans were against it and President Wilson had been re-elected because of the slogan, *"Wilson kept us out of war!"* The Monroe doctrine that proclaimed independence for the Western Hemisphere also informed the Europeans that the U.S. could not interfere in their affairs.

However, Wilson did declare war and the labor papers claimed that the munitions barons, who stood to reap millions, had prevailed. The propaganda of the country's leading newspapers, which, according to the laborites, needed the favors of their capitalist owners, convinced the populace of the need to aid the beleaguered allies. Uncle Sam began to ferry troops across the Atlantic in support of Britain and France against Germany. Good Americans of German decent began to be harassed because of the origin of their names.

At this time Ralph was doing editorial work for Solidarity, one of the larger labor papers. It and other such papers protested loud and clearly. Ralph was a very vocal leader of these. He registered for the draft, but wrote the words, *"opposed to this war"*, under his signature. Other popular laborite leaders such as Eugene Debbs, Bill Haywood and Frank Little were equally opposed. They stuck to their position that our becoming entangled in this conflict was a camouflaged effort to strengthen the position of the war profiteers and international moneylenders.

The eventual result was that all were arrested on a charge of sedition. They had gone on record as having denounced the war as another capitalist slaughterfest.

The war at home now was against the unions and strikes were denounced as aid and comfort to the Kaiser. There were raids throughout the country to roundup so called seditious leaders and about a hundred sixty were netted including the five Solidarity organizers under the banner of Industrial Workers of the World.

They were arraigned for many crimes but principally on counts of sedition. The five of whom Ralph was one were educated men who never had been arrested for crimes of any sort unless claiming the right to free speech was one.

Eugene V. Debs

Ralph was handcuffed to a well-known singer, George Andreychine. Society debutantes from Chicago's Gold Coast offered to chauffeur the prisoners to Cook County Jail in the downtown area in their swank cars as their contribution to the War Bond effort. The two men, along with a guard were put into the back seat of a classy limousine. Two elegant and snooty young women, preening for the press pictures, were to drive. On the way they began a conversation in French airing their views on their *"crumby"* passengers. When they had finished, George spoke to Ralph in perfect French, for he was a man of culture, of the crude morals and manners of Chicago Society girls. They had the comfort of observing two very red necks in front.

Bill Haywood

At the jail the men were assigned to temporary quarters, told to disrobe and put their clothes through the bars for delousing, a true indignity. In his book, Ralph has written that he has never forgotten the creak of the cell doors closing or the cell stench of filth and creosote. They hadn't been there very long when they decided to do some thing about those dirty cells. This was accomplished by persuasion and threats to the head jailor who finally and reluctantly provided them with pails, soaps and brushes. They had the time at least and set about scrubbing the cells thoroughly.

Their next step was to arrange for a program of calisthenics for their exercise periods outside, as there happened to be an instructor among them. Time dragged and they came up with the idea of starting educational meetings for weekdays. The larger groups consisted of miners, loggers, agricultural workers, railroad men and such. A spokesman from each group began to enlighten the others on his trade and its importance to the country.

They decided on a change of pace for Sundays after chapel and implemented an entertainment period, as there were many talented men among them. They worked on a program sheet, which was circulated from cell to cell each week announcing titles such as Anecdotes by Ashley, Duets by Azur and Rey, Poetry recitations, songs etc.

Bill Haywood was a favorite for he really could keep them in suspense and gales of laughter with the tales he told.

They had gone to jail in September and winter gave way to spring before they were charged. Ralph wrote of the long sleepless nights and of his longing for Edith and young son, Vonnie. One such night he found a space on the graffiti filled wall to write a poem, the rhythm of which began to beat in his head, to use his words. He called it *Mourn Not the Dead* and it became the first of his book of prison poems.

Mourn not the Dead that in the cool earth lie
Dust to dust.
The calm, sweet earth that mothers all who die
As all men must.

Mourn not your captive comrades who must dwell
Too strong to strive,
Each in his steel-bound coffin of a cell
Buried alive.
But rather mourn the apathetic throng,
That cowed and the meek
Who see the world's great anguish and its wrong?
And dare not speak.

During the long months in Cook County jail Ralph felt that if they ever were tried they would be acquitted. Sympathizers, many very wealthy liberals among them, were collecting a great many influential people on the outside were working for their release and large sums of bail money.

The happy day of release finally arrived in April and Edith and Vonnie met Ralph at the gate with joyous embraces. He would have a taste of freedom and the outside world had never looked so good. Ralph really felt the need to go back into the studio to help Edith to work for that little dream house in the country but that was impossible at first. Speaking dates had been set up for him and it was his duty to fulfill them. He set out almost at once for Omaha, Kansas City, The Twin Cities, Denver, and the first really big meeting in Seattle where there was much enthusiasm and huge collections resulted. He said later that the loggers were the most underpaid, the toughest, but also the most generous. The National Defense Committee was very much alive.

Still they awaited trial and there was time to look for that little cottage which they found in Lombard, Illinois, about twenty miles from the great metropolis and served by commuter trains.

There was a pretty little house on two acres of ground on the outskirts of the village in which I lived as a young girl. It wasn't very far from our home.

The trial began in April 1918. Kennesaw Mountain Landis, a strongly anti-union judge was to officiate. Leading newsmen from all over the country came to report it. Ralph recognized Carl Sandburg and Ben Hecht between the Chicago contingent and also saw Ben Karsner and cartoon artist, Art Young, from the prominent Labor paper, the New York Call. The trial was to drag along for five months and came to an abrupt end in August 30th, 1918.

The prosecutor took less than an hour to appeal to the jury for conviction and the defendants lawyers decided to rest the case without further argument. Ralph wrote that the jurors, weary as they must have been, certainly were fast workers! I quote from his book, *"In less than an hour they considered the testimony of scores of witnesses covering thousands of specific offences, hundreds of exhibits, as well as some forty thousands pages of typewritten records! That, in addition to consigning almost a hundred men to a total of almost 100 years in prison."* The verdict was guilty as charged. It was Ralph's thirty-first birthday.

Judge Landis meted out sentences a few at a time, starting at one or two years in prison through eight, ten, etc., until he came to the organizers and editors when maximum sentences of twenty years in prison at Leavenworth, Kansas were handed out. Ralph and Bill Haywood also were fined $30,000.00.

What hurt most was that he wasn't allowed to say goodbye to Edith and Vonnie. That same day he was handcuffed to friend, Herbert Mahler, taken to La Salle Street Station and put aboard the waiting special train with many others. He asked for pencil and paper and scribbled a note to Edith in an attempt to reassure her. They eventually reached the Kansas border; he looked out at the landscape and thought sadly that these were the same green rolling prairies that his people had seen so long ago on the wagon train journey to Cloud County.

World War I, the war to end all wars! It had been considered the bloodiest war ever fought until that time and there still were many questions as to whether the United States should ever have been a participant.

Leavenworth Prison was a small world in itself. An effort was made to classify prisoners as to skills and former trades. Ralph had been a commercial artist and was assigned to the finger print office. He became most interested in the technical problems raised by the instruction books. He was entrusted with a precision pen and ink work details and developed skill in detecting frauds, so was able to save at least two suspects whose fingerprints had been doctored.

Ralph was given special privileges when the warden discovered that he could paint. This warden had men in the carpenter shop of the prison making hand carved dining room furniture for his personal use. He decided to take advantage of Ralph's reputation as an artist and brought some of his favorite prints to him with the request that he copy them. The Warden bought canvas and paints and Ralph was pleased to comply.

All liked one of the prisoners, called, Happy, for his sweet disposition. He was a devout Catholic and often served the priest at Sunday masses. He saw the pictures that Ralph was painting for the warden and one day he brought a faded lithograph of Jesus and asked if Ralph could make a life sized copy of it. Ralph agreed to do it but there was the question of procuring the proper materials. Finally he decided to take some of the warden's supplies and turned out a beautiful picture of Jesus. I.W.W. workers within the prison carpenter shop made a splendid oak frame for it and placed it above the Chapel door. It was much admired.

The Warden was angry for, since it was done with his materials, he wanted to keep it. He accused Ralph of stealing the canvas and a short term in solitary was the penalty. The painting was allowed to remain and it gave solace to many penitents as they entered the Chapel.

In 1922 Edith had made a collection of her husband's poems and had them printed in a small book with the help of popular writer Scott Nearing and his wife. Scott also wrote the foreword. The book was called Bars and Shadows and it really took off in sales so that it went to three printings nationally and was widely circulated in Europe because of an English edition sponsored by Storm Jamison, a British author. The prison poems were making many friends for amnesty pleas and Edith wrote her husband that letters were pouring in from all parts of this country and the world.

It was around this time that I was working a summer job and often was on the commuter train with Edith who was a friend of the family by then, a woman whom we all admired and liked. She rode into Chicago daily to her studio work and usually picked up her mail on the way with a stop at the Post Office. That gave her a chance to read her letters enroute. Sometimes Ralph would include poems with his letters and she would share them with me.

Edith was a very warm and friendly young person, petite in a trim little suit and with hat and gloves, pretty and very interesting. She loved the cottage and was making it a home with special attention to lawn and garden areas. She often spoke of her longing for her husband and of their son Vonnie who attended lower grades in the grammar school. He was cared for by his grandfather, Ralph's father, a widower, who made his home with them. She explained that Vonnie could not understand why his father didn't come home as other boy's fathers did and she mentioned her sadness at the way he had clung to his father when he left for Leavenworth. That was the morning that she read me the poem about him, which had been enclosed, in her letter. She was emotional and I, too, felt the tears as I listened.

The Ralph Chaplin Story

To My Little Son

I cannot lose the thought of you.
It haunts me like a song.
It blends with all I see or do
Each day the whole day long.
The train, the lights, the engine's throb
And that stinging memory.
Your brave smile broken with a sob
Your face pressed close to me.
Lips trembling far too much to speak,
The arms that would not come undone,
The kiss so salty on your cheek,
The long, long trip begun.
I could not miss you more it seems
But now I don't know what to say.
It's harder that I ever dreamed
With you so far away.

The movement for amnesty was growing stronger every day. The poems were being printed in the daily papers and an open letter to President Harding had been circulated and widely pushed by many celebrities such as Rodger Baldwin, Robertson Trowbridge and, of course, the American Civil Liberties Union. Ralph had been asked to do pen and ink sketches of prison life for publication. The spring brought many visitors to Leavenworth. Destiny was about to play its part again.

Ralph was working in the Rose Garden, which bordered the shrubs in the yard of the prison hospital when the commutation papers arrived with the signature of President Warren G. Harding. What a joyous day. The freed men could leave at once, Ralph and fourteen others. Hasty good-byes were said and before the day was over they had scattered in many directions.

To Ralph that long train ride to Lombard seemed endless.

There was time for reappraisal and intensified appreciation of American values. As the train raced near the borders of his native state, Kansas, he realized that he was one with its people that his roots went more deeply into its good rich soil than he ever had realized.

It was difficult to adjust to freedom at first, after nearly four years, including those long months in Cook County Jail, although he basked in the love of his wife and son as well as his father. Many friends welcomed him and the mail was filled with congratulations letters. Messages came from all over America and even from Europe and South America.

Even the first lady of the land, Mrs. Harding, remembered Ralph for on White House stationery, the wife of the president wrote a gracious note in which she expressed her happiness that the little Chaplin family was together again. There had been a rumor that she was touched by Ralph's poetry and tales of his beautiful chapel painting at Leavenworth and had helped to bring about his freedom by interceding with her husband. Sadly, a note of condolence went to Mrs. Harding a few weeks later for while he was away on a trip, the president died. Later the Chaplin's were present, as I was, as part of a large crowd of Lombardians assembled beside the old Northwestern depot as we paid our respects on the passage of the black-draped funeral train which carried the remains of President Warren G. Harding.

The following poems are from Bars and Shadows by Ralph Chaplin:

When Death Comes

> *Beauty and joy, I've had too much of both*
> *To grovel now for life's last meager crumbs,*
> *Cringing and bent*
> *I want to face Death boldly when she comes,*
> *With all my powers flaming and unspent,*
> *Still fertile with seeds of future growth*

And discontent.

*I would not have my heart beat overlong
And flutter weakly to its final rest
Withered and cold;
I want to feel it hot within my breast,
A wild clean thing unsullied and unsold,
Pulsing with ecstasies of unborn song
As it did of old.*

*When Death comes I would greet her as a bride
And read the strange enigma of her glance
And understand …
Still young enough to smile and take a chance
I bring her gifts – to take her hand
Thrilling with dreams – and saunter at her side
Into a quiet land.*

Night in the Cell-house

*Tier over tier they rise to dizzy heights
The cells of men who know the world no more.
Silence intense from ceiling to the floor;
While through the window gleams a lone blue light
Which stab the dark immensity of night.
Felt shod and ghostly like a shade of yore
The guard comes shuffling down the corridor;
His key ring jingles … and he glides from sight.*

*Oh, to forget the prison and its scars,
And meet the breeze where ocean meets the land,
To watch the foam crests dance with silver stars
While long green waves come tumbling on the sand …
My brow is hot against the icy bars;
There is a smell of iron on my hand.
Seven Little Sparrows*

Beyond the deep cut window
  The bars are heaped with snow
And seven little sparrows
  Are sitting in a row.

Fluffy blur of snowflakes
  Dappled haze of light;
The narrow prison vista
  Is all awhirl with white.

Seven little sparrows
  Ruffled brown and gray
Snuggled close against the bars
  And this is Christmas.

To Edith

Do you remember how we walked that night
In early spring?
And how we found a new and sweet delight
In everything?
Do you remember how the air was filled
With mist and moonlight - how our hearts were thrilled
And seemed to sing?

What if these walls shut out the world for me
And heaven, too,
There still lives fragrant in my memory
The thought of you.
And out there now with life's tall dome above you
If you but knew how very much I love you –
If you but knew –

Song of Separation

Two that I love must live alone
Far away.
All in the world I can call my own
Only they.
Mother and son in a rocking chair
Thinking of one who cannot be there
Breathing a hope that is half a prayer;
Night and day, night and day.

Here in my cell I must sit alone
Clothed in gray
Bars of iron and walls of stone
Bid me stay.

What of the world with is pomp and show?
Baubles of nothing! This I know;
Deep in my heart I miss them so,
Night and day, night and day.

Some day a silent guard will come for me
And touch my shoulder, surely soon or late;
And lead me to the massive prison gate
And swing it wide and tell me I am free.
Will all this pass, in the days to be?
These nightmare walls, this iron gate of hate?
Or will their shadow always lie in wait
To chill the flame of every ecstasy?

Shall I be cold from living long with death
Like one grave-wrapped, returning from the dead –
My heart a stone – the dungeon on my breath?
Or shall I thrill with sudden awe instead
And feel the terrible and strange delight
Of one long blind who is restored to sight?

WHERE DO WE GO FROM HERE?

The element of mystery makes that a most intriguing question. However, before attempting an answer, I'd like to devote some time to reviewing where we've been in this fantastically productive century.

I came on the scene two and a half years after it began, and have observed most of it with great awareness as the daughter of a journalist father who witnessed and reported on the first half of it. It was as if we had our own anchorman at the dinner table a whole generation before radio and television. My young parents had been on their honeymoon in Buffalo and Niagara Falls in the year 1901 when President William McKinley was assassinated there, and Vice President Theodore Roosevelt was sworn in as President. He had played a part in the Spanish American War, which had recently ended.

Those were the days of horse drawn vehicles, gas light fixtures, and kerosene table lamps. Street cleaners were most important city workers. Electricity had made its appearance and was beginning to operate formerly horse drawn streetcars. Primitive telephones were coming into use but few homes had them yet. Marconi had invented his wireless machines, which were patented in 1896, so telegraph offices were springing up in the cities to carry messages quickly to distant points. They were becoming especially important to newspapers, plentiful then, as they were enabled to print news from distant parts of the country in record time.

Coal stoves, some very fancy ones with isinglass windows, heated houses. Kitchens had iron ranges with built-in boilers and wide ovens. They could be fired with either coal or wood and were excellent room warmers as well.

Toilet facilities even in cities were in small outhouse buildings in back yards. Water came from pumps and was brought to the surface usually by hand pumps, although most towns had downtown fountains from which the busy horses drank. Ice in summer was delivered by dripping wagons and often could be found surrounded by children eager to suck the chips as the ice was cut.

My memory comes alive, so to speak, around age five when we lived in Oklahoma City, which was to be chosen State Capital in 1907. I first heard the word "politics" around that time, for my young father had been lured away from his newspaper job to become Press Chairman for the Republican Party to cover the Constitutional Convention of the new state.

This was convened in Gutherie to settle such matters as redivision of counties, the locations of county seats, such issues as Jim Crow and the liquor traffic, and also to nominate the first governor. Jake Hamon, who later discovered oil and became a multimillionaire, was in charge. He was to become famous, or infamous, in the 1920's Teapot Dome scandal in the Harding administration.

The battles were on between the Democrats and the Republicans, and at times led to physical expressions in the angry tossing of inkbottles at the heads of opponents. Politics were just as dirty in those days as in our recent campaign. The Democrat, Haskell, became the first governor, but Father must have done a good job, for later Haskell wrote him a letter asking him to work for their party. Father declined for he had had his fill of politics and press gentry, and returned to his reporting.

I saw my first motion pictures around that time, if they could be called that. My paternal grandparents came to visit us and stayed to start a small movie theater. I have pictures of that, with Grandpa standing outside and Grandma, barely visible, in the ticket window. He operated the projection machine so I saw almost the first flickers in black and white. I don't remember any of the stories, but they ran ads between films and I do remember a huge loaf of bread on the screen and a big bread knife was slicing it all by itself. The venture was a success, but Grandma was plagued by rheumatism and felt that the Oklahoma climate was causing it, so they sold out and returned to Memphis. The family often has wondered if that was missed opportunity.

However, shortly afterward Father joined the young Associated Press *(now one of the world's leading news services)*, and we were moved to St. Louis. He had a great sense of history, and when there was a special event of interest he made it a point to take my sister, a year younger, and me to witness it.

One such occasion was in about 1910 when the first airplane races were held in St. Louis. The planes, practically crates with wings, seats for two open to the breezes, performed stunts flying not too far from the grandstands. My remembered impressions are that they were very noisy, quite frightening, but very exciting

President Teddy Roosevelt had taken his first plane ride the day before, had removed his big western hat, grabbed a tweed cap from the head of a reporter, placed it on his own head, beak backwards, and climbed aboard. Father was that reporter, and needless to say, that cap became a household souvenir.

We were transferred to Des Moines after a year or two and once again our grades were interrupted, for those changes never came at the beginning of the school year! Father opened the first Associated Press office in Des Moines and met many interesting arrivals to that city. One was Norwegian Captain Ronald Amundson, discoverer of the South Pole. That had been a recent event and he was touring with a slide show of his adventures, hoping to make money toward a rescue trip for a missing explorer. We were taken to see it and later we met the great explorer. He was still standing beside his projection machine, and he said something in accented English, put his hands lightly on our heads and presented us with picture cards of penguins, which he said were the first ever seen in North America. I still have mine.

Another interesting event comes to mind. We were taken to see the famous evangelist, Billy Sunday, a former big league baseball player. He stood on a platform at the front of a huge tent with sawdust covering the aisle floors. Billy wound up as if to pitch a ball but really pitched his sermon, drove it home with other gestures, caught the imaginary return ball with an *"Out!"* for Satan. His gestures were amusing but pertinent and his voice loud and clear. A big organ stood at one side, and the talented Rhodheaver played solo at times or accompanied a great choir. At the end, he played marching music as the congregation was invited to the sawdust trail for Billy's blessing. Father had to leave so we *"hit"* the trail, in the opposite direction.

Meanwhile, time was passing and cars were coming along to send horses back to the barns. My first ride in a car was with a Des Moines neighbor who took her daughter to school in an *"electric,"* a box-like affair that had a bar across the driver's seat for steering. It had room for four or five passengers and was very nicely upholstered. It traveled along very smoothly and quietly.

By that time homes were being fitted with electric light fixtures, often beside the old gas ones, and gas ranges were replacing the coal stoves in the kitchens. I lived only in cities, and apartment buildings had furnaces instead of coal stoves by the time World War I was brewing. It began in Europe in 1914 and we entered in 1917, and our first warplanes began to fly. I graduated from Chicago's Walter Scott grammar school that year and the boys in the class performed the play, *Man Without a Country* and my artist girl friend and I wrote and directed a set of tableaus on war nursing. We had made our graduation dresses, white middies and skirts of poplin material, and they were most appropriate as costumes for the sketches.

The earliest talking machines were on the scene

when I arrived, the ones with the tulip-shaped horns, and my grandpa had one, but the later, greatly improved phonographs played an important role in teen-age lives as I grew up. Our first was an Edison that played thick, unbreakable records with a diamond needle. A few years later we bought a Brunswick, which was a joy for it played not only Edison's but also Victors as well as Brunswick records, each with a different needle. My parents favored classical music, but we kids loved dance music and kept up with the new ones and thought of the phonograph as the most important household fixture.

The first radios began to appear in the 1920's. A neighbor and friend made the first set we heard and, in the summer, placed it near an open window near the street so that passers-by could enjoy any program that happened to be relayed. Often these were quite sporadic. Radio stations were getting started, however, and talented musicians, singers, and other entertainers were invited to audition and to perform, without pay, if they wished. Many enjoyed doing that. Small earphone sets began to be made and sold.

Politics always had a front seat at our dinner table, and in the Twenties the very corrupt Harding administration was making daily headlines and was being discussed in all of its angles. Jake Hamon, now very rich in oil wells, was an important party man. As I mentioned earlier, Father had known him quite well in Oklahoma during the *"Con-Con"* days before his wealth, and he ran into him at some of the Republican gatherings. They had lunch together and had a fine time discussing the good ol' days.

When they were parting, Father asked for a tip as to who would be the next president. Hamon hesitated and then said quietly that Warren G. Harding had been chosen and was a sure bet, as Cox and Franklin Roosevelt, as well as Socialist Eugene Debbs and a Farmer Labor Party candidate would oppose him. He was right, and Debbs pulled more than a million votes that year.

Harding was the owner of an Ohio newspaper and he brought a number of his cronies into office. They certainly were not of statesman quality and it wasn't long before scandal was brewing in high places such as the Departments of Justice and the Interior. It involved the selling of public lands to private concerns in the oil business, and became known as the Teapot Dome Scandal. President Harding died suddenly on a vacation trip to the West, and Vice President Calvin Coolidge succeeded him. The lengthy trials were left to him and some jail sentences resulted. Since Father had been seen talking to Jake Hamon, he was subpoenaed to the Senate hearings, but could add nothing.

The Twenties brought on the so-called *"flapper"* age among women who had become active in the Women's Movement for equal rights. They were enfranchised to vote along with their husbands, and began to claim other privileges. Irene and Vernon Castle became very popular dancers in those years, and Irene even dared to cut off her long hair! That drew gossip and disapproval, but really started a fad, which began to catch on. Clothing for women had become less austere and skirts no longer swept the floors as the nation discovered that women had legs! I had always been sort of an independent soul, as I was athletic and could run faster in the schoolyards than any of my girl friends. I had never worn a corset of any kind and couldn't understand how my little mother could wrap herself in those things with horrible stays, for I would have felt imprisoned.

I had hip-long hair and one day when I was eighteen I went to a barbershop on impulse and had it cut off. It felt so good to shake my head and feel hair really move! My folks didn't scold, although my mother kept that bundle of hair, but I was amazed to find that some of my girl friends' mothers were angry.

By the late Twenties radio manufacturing was in full swing. We could keep up with the news almost as soon as it happened, hear great music and enjoy dramatic productions, such fifteen-minutes series as Vic and Sade, The Goldberg's, Mary Martin, wonderful Kate Smith, and much of America went to bed after listening to Amos and Andy.

Airplanes had been greatly improved and the Post Office adopted them to facilitate the delivery of mail. The great Charles Lindbergh became one of the pilots. He later distinguished himself by flying The Spirit of St. Louis across the Atlantic, solo. That was in 1927. Movies in black and white had been a way of life for a number of years, and they and newsreels had helped to shrink the size of the world as we became familiar with lifestyles in Europe, Asia, Africa and most other areas.

Unhappily, the catastrophic stock market crash ushered in the Thirties. The worst in history, it nearly brought America to her knees. Banks failed almost daily all across the country, and life savings of millions were lost. Businesses went bankrupt and employees became jobless. There also had been several years of extreme drought in the Midwest and South, and dustbowl conditions were driving thousands from their homes. *"Brother can you spare a dime?* Became the theme song of that period when people actually were on the city streets selling apples for a dime.

I was married and living in Lombard, Illinois, a Chicago suburb, with a husband and two little boys. We were fortunate to have a half-acre lot and, as my husband's company was hanging on by its teeth, rotating workers a week on and a week off, he finally had time to do his beloved gardening. He raised elegant sweet corn and tomatoes, as well as many other vegetables. We ate well and supplied relatives and friends, also. It was a time of canning and preserving and much other unpaid work.

Life went on, and we had little money but felt lucky instead of poor. Butter was a quarter a pound, less on sale, meat and other supplies were equally cheap. Gas tanks could be practically filled for a dollar. We attended very excellent movies for a quarter apiece, and sometimes even got a free dish! Most of our friends were in the same boat, and we continued to have bridge parties with dime store prizes, and there were times when we even splurged to serve boiled shrimps with hot sauce dips for snacks. They could be had for 35 cents a pound.

All looked forward to President Roosevelt's wonderful fireside chats on radio. He usually ended them on a positive note that left us feeling confident and hopeful. His first one declared a bank holiday, which helped to stem the chaotic slide of failing banks and the people knew that at least something was being done.

As time passed, many programs were set up to aid the jobless, who simply could not find jobs for they were non-existent. The Roosevelt administration set up such services as the Civilian Conservation Corps to get young men off the streets by sending them to camps across the country to do needed work in forests or wherever. They were paid thirty dollars a month and received board, as the Army did. Many of them sent the money home to their families. The WPA and NRA, and subsidy programs for artists and musicians, came into being, and in 1935, the Social Security Trust Fund, it was a people-oriented era.

The Depression was a very long ordeal, and it took our entry into World War II to begin improvements. Munitions factories started up and related businesses began again. Sadly, our young men were being sent off to distant shores once more. Douglas Aircraft was making DC-3's for the Army and some of my women friends went to work for them. As the shortage of employable men grew, great numbers of women went into unfamiliar working areas, and many stayed in the new fields after the war ended.

The country finally was getting back to full productivity when the bombing of Hiroshima, Japan brought the war to an abrupt end in August of 1945. An American plane dropped that first atomic bomb and the death and destruction toll was horrendous. President Roosevelt missed that, for he had died earlier that year and President Truman was sworn in.

President Franklin Roosevelt, the only one to be elected four times, had seemed ill when he was in Yalta to sign the treaty with allies Winston Churchill and Russia's, Joseph Stalin. Sadly for me, my own father died suddenly on March 24, 1945 at age 68. He had worked that day as editor of The Suburban Times of Des Plaines and, so to speak, died with his boots on, as he would have wished. President Roosevelt died a couple of weeks later on April 12th, at Warm Springs, Georgia. Two other very prominent leaders in World War II, Adolph Hitler and his mistress, committed suicide, and the Italians murdered Mussolini and his Clara Petachi, also in April. It has been my fancy that Father went into the Hereafter first to be on hand for their dramatic arrivals, as any good newsman would wish to cover those!

The earliest television in black and white began to appear in the late Forties and sales took a huge leap in the Fifties. Teenagers often gathered at the homes of friends lucky enough to have a set, and soon began to nag their parents to buy one. No one realized in those early days the enormous effect that TV would have on our life and times!

The world seemed to be living at a more hectic pace and the Sixties brought changes, challenges, and drama. They also became the backdrop for another horrible war, which was opposed by many. Once again, our young men were being siphoned off to fight great distances from home, across the Pacific to Vietnam. The college generation began to rebel and to pull away from the manners and mores of the past, including the accepted moral codes. The great Civil Rights movement, long overdue, began in the South, partly triggered by the action of Rosa Parks who refused to sit in the back of the bus, to which blacks were assigned. The Reverend Martin Luther King led his people in rebellion, and there were many marches to proclaim their rights under the Constitution and for which the Civil War had been fought.

There was a memorable walk to Washington by thousands of blacks and sympathetic whites. All of these demonstrations were not enough, and this natural orator and leader was assassinated in Memphis, Tennessee, where he had gone to make his famous speech which began with the words, *"I have a dream..."*

The Sixties were marred by another tragedy in the assassination of President John F. Kennedy, our youngest and a very popular one. He was on a trip to Dallas, Texas, for a political speaking event.

This all happened before the eyes of the world, for Television brought the dramatic story to all in detail, and America remained glued to the Tube as the sad story unfolded from the actual shooting, confirmation from the hospital, the swearing-in of Vice President Lyndon Johnson with his wife and Mrs. Kennedy beside him, the flight back to Washington on Air Force One with the coffin aboard, the services there, and I particularly remember the walk of Mrs. Kennedy and the procession of international diplomats from the Capitol to the church, for the head of very tall Charles De Gaulle, in the splendor of military attire, towered above all others. Also, very sad and unforgettable, was the horse-drawn caisson bearing the casket, and the traditional riderless horse, carrying the unsheathed sword and with boots on backwards. We even saw the lighting of the perpetual torch by Mrs. Kennedy.

The Seventies were highlighted by another of our political scandals in the Watergate affair, which led to the resignation of President Nixon, who was close to impeachment. I was, as is usual for me, following the story closely with much interest when, right at the climax, my dear husband of nearly fifty years died of a heart attack. That was on the 4th of August 1974, so I never think of one without remembering the other.

One really good thing happened in the Seventies, for the unwinnable Vietnam War came to a close and our surviving lads were brought home. Of course, there were many major accomplishments during the 70's, computers had been introduced, astronauts were exploring outer space, and technology had produced all sorts of new and improved gadgets.

Almost before we realized it, the eighties were upon President Carter's and us. Four years were ending. We were about to elect a Republican by an overwhelming vote. He had once been movie actor, Ronald Reagan, and more recently, Governor of California. He has been one of our most popular presidents and seemingly can do no wrong in the eyes of the public. However, some of the cronies he brought into office with him have been less than statesman-like and have lacked ethics. They have been a disappointing lot, who were more interested in lining their own pockets than in good government.

America was composed of immigrant populations from many countries and cultures at the turn of the century. There were floods of newcomers later, but a large population of truly ethnic Americans had begun to emerge. They were the result of the fused bloodlines, principally European, of these early arrivals. Many inherited the talents and skills of those ancestors.

At first they had been anxious to work at anything and they put in terribly long hours for very low pay while crafty employers enriched themselves. Eventually they became wise and began to band together to demand a decent pay scale for those endless hours of labor. Their organizations would later be called labor unions and they survived to become powerful, sometimes through bloodshed and agony.

The early machine trades, carpenters, boilermakers, etc., set standards of excellence and the young men who wished to work in them had an apprenticeship of three years before they were entitled to top pay, but then they were situated for life in a good employment field.

In this way the middle class was born and, with multi-

additions from many other fields became the backbone of America. The businesses and corporations derived a decent profit, if not the exorbitant sums of the early exploiters.

Because he earned a livable wage, the man of the house was able to support his family alone while his wife, mother of his children, stayed home to nurture them and to teach her brood. She saw them off to school, took them to church, and expected them to study, which they did. Many of these students grew up to be the teachers, scientists inventors, writers and historians of their times. They appeared to have a good life, invented their own fun, and helped to make America great.

Sweeping changes throughout the world have been underway much of this century. Russia became Communist after the Revolution in 1917. Later, the Asian countries revolted against entrenched monarchistic rulers, and China, under the Communist leadership of Mao Tse Tung closed her doors to the outside world.

I remember that when we first heard of the Communist revolution, and among other facts, that women as well as men would be required to work outside the home, we wondered about the children. The government would provide nurseries and preschool homes and would train people to care for them. We thought that they would be deprived, for there could be no better place than with mother at home!

Now, America has had a decade of union busting and corporate takeovers and thousands of decent jobs have disappeared. The antitrust laws have been set aside, and we see, almost daily, huge corporate takeovers of large firms and sometimes many firms, usually on credit. The turn of the century robber barons at least left such things as railroads, mines, or meatpacking houses, but the new breed just stockpiles profits. Many men and women who have made careers with the companies and felt that they were secure for life now find themselves seeking other employment. Their mortgages were suitable to the good wages they had enjoyed, but the minimum paying jobs, even with both working, are not sufficient, particularly with the necessity to pay for day care for the little children. Their older children become *"the latchkey kids."*

The national debt of America is measured in the trillions area, double the amount accumulated by all previous administrations together. There are more millionaires and billionaires than ever before, and many thousands more of street people. Joblessness matches that in the Depression era of the Thirties. The factories that have been taken to other countries, such as now-prosperous Korea, were moved there because of cheap wages such as a dollar an hour for garment workers. The profits go to the owners, but the taxes go to the other countries. The rich of many countries have been buying large buildings or other huge chunks of the U.S. Among them are Japan, England, Germany, the oil rich of the Middle East, etc.

The selling of America certainly may alter our economic position in the world. Even presidential candidate Gebhardt said in one of his talks that we are losing our share of America and that our standard of living is dropping.

There was a recent newspaper story on the loss of farms across our land, some 140,000 of them. Some had been taken over by powerful conglomerates, but the rest were simply gone! Also, there are 85,000 more set for foreclosure. They have been given some extra time to come up with payments in the hope that they can be saved.

In the cities a third of the thousands of homeless have jobs that don't pay enough to provide homes, so they live in buses, cars, tents, shacks, etc. A recent Charles Kuralt Sunday morning show covered a number of those with interviews and graphic photographs. A sad commentary!

A vast domestic change of course is beginning to emerge. Where do we go from here? Of course, we have another decade in which to prepare to meet the 21st century. Let us devoutly hope that many of the most depressing problems can be addressed and corrected by that time!

First, we had better try to save our planet or nothing else will matter! That will concern all nations, for all of the oceans, lakes, and rivers are belching up the filth of centuries of dumping wastes into them. The horribly contaminated waters are killing fish and other creatures, as well as vegetation. The survivors are unfit to eat, and much of the world needs that food.

On that list also is the greenhouse effect on Mother Earth. The term is used to describe a condition caused by the buildup of carbon dioxide, methane and other gases in the atmosphere. They act as an insulator and cause the earth's temperature to rise. Those gases are destroying the ozone layer that screens out ultraviolet rays of the sun. An increase of those rays causes skin cancers and even seems to suppress the immune system of the body.

Of course, there is the terrible pollution of the earth itself. We continue to manufacture and stockpile such products as the plutonium triggers for weapons at nearby Rocky Flats. Deadly wastes are accumulating daily, and there is no place to bury them. The earth surrounding that area, and probably the waters below, are so contaminated that they probably cannot be cleaned up for most of a century.

We have other worries than the debt and pollution of our precious earth. They reach our children through the enormous drug problem in this country, which has filtered down to them. Our young have been deprived of the once long and happy period of growing up. They have become entangled in sex far too soon, and have been exposed to all sorts of distorted emotions by television and movies. The restrictive moral codes of the past have vanished and many young minds have been turned away from schooling. There are far too many dropouts. It seems that America has dropped behind other countries in education, which is first in importance in Asia, Russia, and most European countries. Our children are our most important assets, and our leaders of the future must be found among them.

Where do we go from here? All signs seem to point toward a technological age and we will leave a marvelous platform from which it can leap. The Xerox copier came along some years ago to revolutionize the printing industry. Calculators, down to pocket size, came along to do our arithmetic. One of the most remarkable finds has been the silicon chip, and computers and word processors came into being. The computer possibilities are just about unlimited and the word processor is making typewriters obsolete, for it can type, spell, correct, file and even spit out copies on demand! It does almost everything but compose its own material.

There have been hundreds of gadgets to make housekeeping easier, and if we wished to stay home for a period of time and had a well-stocked freezer, we could live comfortably indefinitely. Local and world news would be brought to us almost as soon as it happened. We could watch movies in lovely color, or listen to our favorite music in stereo sound. We could cook good meals in minutes in our microwave ovens, and washing would be no problem, for we could just toss our clothes in the washer, turn on the tap and forget it. We could thoroughly clean our carpets with our vacuum cleaners in a short time. Shades of the old carpet beater and the many hours of beating it as it was draped over the backyard clothesline in the spring! We have been so blessed!

Even greater such blessings are in store for the 21st century, it seems, for according to the gist of a story I heard this week on television, the steel used in construction today will be replaced by much lighter and stronger glass fiber! Robots that will do the work of former blue-collar workers will manufacture it. Houses will be built of the material at the factories, lifted full-grown from the lots by small blimps, and placed on the property of the buyer.

Education will be doubly important, and two-thirds will

increase the numbers of teachers. Originality and use of the imagination will be required, and workers will be combining several of their talents where possible. For instance, the talent for music might also indicate one in art or the graphic arts. We would then be required to use either or both. Medical studies will uncover cures for many of the former killer diseases, and people will continue to live longer and healthier lives.

Along with Russia, which sent the first cosmonaut, Yuri Gagarin, into outer space and which now has established a space station, the United States has made great strides in space travel, and we have walked on the moon! Dr. Louis Freedman suggests that we could combine efforts in the exploration of outer space and allow crews to fly tandem to Mars, and even that a multi-national effort in that direction could include Japan and other nations.

Isaac Asimov writes in the December 17th Time magazine, *"...the teaming earth? Colonize the moon! Build space stations. Then go on to populate Mars and other planets. There is unlimited solar energy and a plethora of minerals and acres of land! We already are more informed about outer space than the early explorers ever were about the oceans they sailed and the lands they discovered."*

If only we could learn to respect each other and end those stupid wars! Century old hates have no reason for continuing in this century. Mother Earth herself is scolding. She's rumbling and grumbling and exploding. She's protesting all of the terrible destruction brought on by the hates of her progeny. She's urging them to quit teaching hate and telling them that their babies are not born hating. That is taught to them. She's proving that the ugly wars and other careless destructions are minor compared to what she can do in the tremendous upheaval of her breast in one earthquake. She's telling us that if we don't quit destroying her, she'll destroy us!

Robert Burns tells the field mouse whose home his plow

has destroyed:

> *"But Mousie, thou are blessed to me.*
> *The present only troubles thee,*
> *But, ach, I backward cast my eye*
> *O'er prospects drear*
> *An' forward though I cannae see,*
> *I guess an' fear.*

PRESIDENTIAL TIMBER

That title provoked considerable thought as you might guess for I have been around for the terms of sixteen presidents. The first was Theodore Roosevelt who was followed by William Howard Taft, the only one I ever saw in person, for he was in a parade in Des Moines when I was about ten and the public schools had been dismissed so that students could line curbs along the route. He sat in one of the primitive cars and seemed to take up most of the back seat as he waved to all the giggly little girls and I thought he was awfully fat!

Next in line was Woodrow Wilson who served from 1913 to 1921 and was reelected because of the slogan; *"Wilson Kept Us Out of War"*. That was world war one that had been fought in Europe since 1914. We were in that war by 1917! Warren Harding was elected in 1921 and served until his sudden death while on a trip West in 1923. He was succeeded by Vice President, Calvin Coolidge, who stayed until 1929, followed by Hoover, Franklin Roosevelt, Truman, Eisenhower, Kennedy, Johnson, Nixon, Ford, Carter, Reagan and Bush.

Most of our presidents had University educations, most often in law that was a stepping stone to Politics, and had held offices as congressman, senators, governors, and judges or in other related fields. Many had business connections or came from very wealthy families. In a recent article I read, that contrary to legends, only three of our presidents were born poor and that means poor by today's standards, not necessarily by those of their times. Though born in a log cabin, Lincoln was in the top fifteen percent of taxpayers in his community. That is, his father was. The majority of presidents came from well-endowed forebears and college degrees from such universities as Harvard, Yale and Princeton, predominated.

Charisma is a word we hear a lot these days as it consists

of good looks, partly, but is made up of the projection of a certain sexual attraction and a good degree of intelligence and energy. Also, it makes people appealing to the opposite sex. TV cameras are able to capture that today, and it is a great help in getting elected.

As I grew up, our history books made great heroes of our founding fathers and little was printed about their private lives. This was partly due to the fact newspapers were too few and too far away in those days before wireless was invented.

Now, with television, radio, cable, a plethora of newspapers and magazines, there is almost too much exposure and a candidate can be destroyed over night as was candidate Gary Hart in the last election. He was almost a babe in the woods in comparison with some of the former presidents I have read about lately.

A book by Marvin Kitman entitled, *The Making of a President* described Washington as a foppish sort of gentleman who loved clothes and the ladies as well as dancing. His passionate letters to Sally Fairfax were well known, but at least eight others played a part.

Thomas Jefferson was socially prominent when he lived in France and loved the ladies. After the death of his wife, he fell in love with the beautiful octoroon slave, Sally Hemings, the half sister of his wife who was sired by his father-in-law. It is said that he had several children by her, some of whom inherited his red hair.

Ben Franklin, co-writer of our constitution, raised an illegitimate son and even described other affairs in his writings. He was a brilliant man, also. President Warren Harding was a handsome, man-about-town sort of person. He was married to an older woman but was known to have extra marital affairs. Then there was John Kennedy, who, especially since his death, has had a lot of publicity on his numerous ladyloves. He was an excellent leader, also, and it was surprising to me to note that, in our recent election, both candidates constantly referred to both Kennedy and Franklin Roosevelt as our greatest recent presidents! Roosevelt also had a lady or two besides his brilliant wife, Eleanor. Most of the above where charismatic, leader types, men with intelligence and ideas.

My story will be about such a man who was entrenched in the politics of the late tens and twenties. He was a staunch Republican who was a very active leader in the 1929 convention in Chicago to nominate Warren Harding for president. I thought of him when I wrote my last essay for Delphian. He was Jacob Hamon who had been in charge of Oklahoma's statehood convention in 1907. My dad worked on that convention as Republican Press Chairman and knew him well then. His was an interesting story so I decided to do a review of a book by Lone Quinby published in 1931.

Jacob Hamon was a law school graduate from the University of Kansas and was married to Georgia Perkins Hamon soon after. They were the parents of two small children, a son named Jacob and a little blond daughter called Olive Belle.

In Oklahoma's wild early days they had pitched a tent on acreage they hoped to homestead near Lawton, Oklahoma. Jake had brought along his lawyer sign and placed it in town among others. He opened a small office, and his wife, carrying a baby on her knee, drove him in their second hand buggy to and from the office, daily.

Jake was anxious to be a big wheel and had great confidence in himself. He intended to be a great lawyer and had the appearance and personality to achieve this. There was competition with other lawyers but he was lucky in the clients he served and soon was on his way to success.

One day Jake walked into a small store to buy some trifle and was waited on by the bookkeeper, a very pretty sixteen-year-old girl named Clara Smith. Small and with a slight and willowy figure, she had startlingly wide and expressive brown eyes. He was captivated by her looks and found the time toward dusk to stop in for some small article quite often. He lingered to chat and began to tell her about himself and his ambitions, even though he still wore rather seedy clothes.

Clara was a good listener and was soon becoming attracted to this stranger who bragged about future adventures and built castles in the air. To others his talks about maybe being president some day and actually living in the White House in Washington were pipe dreams by an egotistical forty-year-old lawyer.

Lawton, Oklahoma in 1910 was the scene of oil discoveries that would make a great many people as rich as Croesus. Many of the relocated Indians, fortunately, benefited as well. They were descendants of the cruelly moved Florida tribes, which was ironic. The town was still filled with tents, men with guns, whiskey and affectionate ladies of the evening. There were the teepees of the Indians interspersed with the small houses that were springing up almost daily. Oil drilling operations had begun and many residents who had arrived on foot or in old buggies began to reap harvests of money. Jake was one of them and was on his way to his first million.

Clara Smith was a warm, friendly girl who had only flirted with the lads of her age and at times with older customers. She had never been in love but was rapidly being dazzled by this interesting, story telling man and she looked forward to his visits.

Jake was not the type to be satisfied by handholding and Clara's mind and coquettish ways enchanted him, as his wife never had done. He began to fancy Clara as the ideal mate to fill his Washington dreams. There, her wit and beauty would match the charms of history's Dolly Madison!

By the time he proposed a relationship, she had fallen in love. She had felt that such a man, saddled with a wife that she visualized as cold comfort both mentally and physically, deserved better. Clara was now seventeen and he was the only man who had ever aroused any desire in her. Also, it was a country of wide-open spaces where questionable alliances were numerous and went practically unnoticed.

Their close relationship began and he arranged further schooling for her so as to have her ready to serve as his secretary. He already had opened a larger office in Ardmore and they went there to live in commuting rooms at Hotel Randel where she eventually became his special hostess as well.

Jake's wife, Georgia, was not unaware of his romance, but she stayed in Lawton to keep the home together and to see to the children's educations. She would wait patiently for him to tire of the affair.

Meanwhile, Jake became more active in politics and was becoming the mastermind of the Oklahoma oil empire as well as the dictator of Republican politics in the state. His name was spreading around in political circles as far as Washington and other parts of the country. He was becoming known as a man of great initiative as well as a genius in organization. In his late forties he had amassed a fortune of five million dollars and his political ambitions were really taking hold. Soon he was to be appointed National Republican Committeeman.

However, as Jake was becoming a figure of national importance, a cloud was beginning to form. His affair with Clara had lasted eight years and had seemed to be genuine love. At sometime over those years, he had arranged a marriage for her with his divorced nephew, Frank Hamon, a marriage of convenience only, for which he paid Frank a hundred dollars a month. Then, with the legal right to his name, Clara could travel with him as his kinswoman and secretary. Now he could keep her beautifully attired in furs and jewels. She became a charming and much admired hostess. Many of those who worked with him knew of the illicit affair and he realized that the breath of scandal could ruin everything. He dreaded it, but finally the time was arriving when he would have to urge Clara to step aside, painful, as that would be.

He saw the handwriting on the wall early in 1919 and began to court his wife. She had received money from him all along, had moved to a lovely home in Fort Worth, Texas, to give the children better educations and had continued her own. She had improved her appearance with fashionable clothing and had grown more attractive with time. She considered Clara a child, almost young enough to be Jake's daughter. She had gone to Clara's mother a few times, but she claimed all was Jake's fault and that she could do nothing. The fact that he also had been generous with money to Clara's family may have made them reluctant to complain.

Jake began to break away from Clara gently, found reasons to travel East alone and visited Georgia as often as possible. He began to be acquainted with his son and daughter, wrote affectionate notes and sent them presents. He was surprised and pleased with his wife's looks and accomplishments. She was quite willing to travel with him on political jaunts and when the Republican National Convention to nominate a president was held in Chicago, he took her along. They stayed at the Sheridan Hotel and walked arm in arm to various meetings. Mrs. Hamon, beautifully gowned and coifed, entertained her husband's friends and gained an enviable reputation as hostess, a lovely and gracious one.

The convention made history in Chicago, especially when the popular Oklahoma oil king and political czar offered the state of Oklahoma up on the platter to nominate Warren G. Harding for president.

Finally, when on November second, Harding won the election; it was conceded that Jacob Hamon, for his support of the Ohio candidate, had won new triumphs for the Republicans. It was rumored that, for this brilliant piece of work, the Oklahoma genius might be appointed the

Secretary of the Interior. Other reports had it that his name had been advanced as a possible dark horse candidate during one of the convention's several deadlocks!

Back in Ardmore, Clara Smith Hamon was truly miserable. She realized that a complete break in her relationship was inevitable. She constantly brooded her fate. She had loved him and worked with him for eight years. In the beginning she had slept with him in crumby hovels and dumps in oil fields as well as later in fine hotels and had played an important part in his career shaping. She still loved him but was being thrown into discard because of his paranoiac ambition. Only twenty-five, she felt old.

It was late November, nearly Thanksgiving. Clara's trunks were packed, filled with mementos of wild, happy days and nights of travels, her diaries full of tales of exciting episodes, passion, heartaches, sad moments, but also of great beauty.

She sat crying, filled with bitterness that all was over. It was twilight and memories still kept flooding. She had been the guardian of political secrets and of powerful business transactions as both sweetheart and secretary. She had had such a full life and now it was empty.

She reached into her purse to get a filmy handkerchief to wipe here eyes and her fingers touched the small revolver that Jake had given her some time back to protect another gift, a ten thousand dollar ring.

Several hours later a powerfully built man with his head bent slightly, stumbled to the Hardy Sanitarium a block away. His arm was linked to that of another man. In a few minutes, Jake Hamon and Doctor Walter Hardy walked in. Jake, whitening, said that he had accidentally shot himself while cleaning a gun. He asked that his business manager be sent for. He was Frank Ketch.

The next morning he still lay in his hospital bed wounded by a bullet that had entered his abdomen on the right side, ranged downward and backward through the right lobe of his liver and stopped just short of the spinal chord. Clara, wearing a veil, was admitted to see him. She left shortly afterward, hurrying down the street toward the office of business manager, Frank Ketch. Jake Hamon died five days later.

We were living in a Chicago suburb and I do remember the black *"extra"* headlines that crowned the papers that night. They were blockbusters! Radio was not yet in general use, but the newsreels in the movie theaters gave graphic pictures and kept us informed as well as newspapers and magazines that were plentiful. Jake Hamon Dies!

A month of stories began. At first the shooting was believed to have been an accident as he had said. Then it came out that Clara Smith Hamon had disappeared!

The body of Jacob Hamon lay in state in the convention hall in Oklahoma attired in the new suit he had bought to wear to the upcoming inauguration. Several thousand people passed his bier, many of them famous, to honor him. Georgia Hamon received messages of condolence from all parts of the country and a cablegram from president-elect, Harding, who was on the U.S. Pastores on his way to Panama.

Now a trap was set to ensnare the missing Clara. There were rumors that political and financial interests had financed her escape. The purpose was thought to be to throw a smoke screen about the whole affair. However, the county attorney had issued a warrant for her arrest. A young reporter was assigned to the case and he finally found that her trunks had been sent to Kansas City. A permit to have them opened was granted, and of course, the diaries were discovered and read. Then the scandal hit the fan!

It took nearly a month to find her and the reporter had traveled five thousand miles, back and forth and round about, before locating her with her young brother in Chicuacua, Mexico. She was very tired of hiding and explained that Jake and his financial advisors had arranged for her to leave at once. He was still living when she left and it was thought he might survive.

She was taken to her sister's home in the oil town of Wilson and her bond was fixed at twelve thousand dollars. She told her side of the story and began with the fact that she had known that Jake would come to bid her good-bye that tragic night. He came late, had been drinking a great deal and was quarrelsome to the point that she was afraid of him. She quietly took her gun from the purse in the dimly lighted room and, holding it in front of her, started to back out the door. He must have thought she was going to shoot, so lifted a chair to bring down on her head. He missed her, but the chair hit the gun that fired! So, neither had pulled the trigger. He slumped to the floor and she called for help.

Dozens of the most important men in the state came forward to sign her bond. One wealthy man offered five hundred thousand dollars toward her defense and there were others who would contribute.

Mrs. Hamon, widow of the slain man, tried to shield his memory and decided to attend the trial. She was bitter toward Clara; understandably, for the girl had broken up her home for years and now had further ruined her family life.

Some witnesses swore that the death was an accident while others, under oath, felt that Clara had shot Jake, for they thought they had his own words for that. The eyes of America were feverishly focused on the trial. Not only the political factions, but also the oil interests and the ordinary citizens throughout the country, opinions were pretty well divided. Gamblers were betting that Clara would not be convicted and many watchers took the stand saying that Jake had not wanted a trial and felt that she had not pulled the trigger.

When the evidence was all in on March 18, 1921, the jury deliberated only thirty-seven minutes to bring in the verdict, *Not Guilty!* Spectators in the courtroom cheered and many rushed to climb over chairs to get to the weeping

Clara to congratulate her. Lone Quinby ends her story with the comment, *"Thus ends one man's vision of the journey to the White House in which two women figured."*

Continuing with my theme, I would like to talk a bit about the man who became president after being nominated that late night by tired senators in a smoke filled hotel room.

Warren Gamaliel Harding was inaugurated shortly after Jake Hamon's demise. An Ohioan, he had attended Ohio Central College. Interested in journalism, he acquired the newspaper, The Marion Ohio Star, and was married to a wealthy widow, Florence Kling De Wolfe. The paper prospered and he became interested in Republican politics and was elected state senator. Later he was lieutenant governor and finally Senator. As he was a speaker of orator caliber, he became Republican keynote speaker in 1916.

Harding was a handsome man who could be quite charming and was most attractive to the ladies who provided considerable romance, it was rumored. He wasn't the brightest president and seemed aware of that, but he was a hard worker and the type to anguish over a decision. Quoting from Richard Schenkman's book on some of the presidents, I find that he once said to his secretary, *"John, I can't make a damn thing out of this tax problem! I listen to one side and that seems right. Then I talk to the other side who seems just as right and, God!, I m back where I started. Dear God, what a job!"*

Some of Harding's appointments were excellent for they included Andrew Mellon, Charles Evans Hughs and Herbert Hoover. Unfortunately, he also appointed a number of his cronies to high office, some of whom were mediocre and others who were down right corrupt! Later that gave rise to a rumor that he was a political stooge. The Teapot Dome scandal began early in his term. That had to do with the give away of public lands to oil interests.

Some of his actions, however, disproved the stooge remarks, for if he thought something right on the other side, he decided in that area. One good thing, I think, was the release of imprisoned Socialist, Eugene Debs, also a former presidential candidate, but who, along with many others, had written and spoken against our entry into World War one. One of our Lombard neighbors, Ralph Chaplin, poet, artist, writer, about whom I wrote in another Delphian essay, also was released at that time.

President Harding left on a vacation trip to Alaska that summer in 1923 and died out west on his way home. The flag-draped funeral train passed through Lombard and I was down at the station with the watching crowd as it moved slowly past. Vice president, Calvin Coolidge, inherited the Big Teapot scandal that was soon to bring, once again, screaming headlines to the newspaper industry. Several men in the highest offices went to prison.

Memory carries me back to those days as I was just finishing high school and found the times interesting and exciting, for we had a newsman father who was reporting the stories and beguiling us at the dinner table with events as they happened. Within less than three years the U.S. had three big scandals beginning with the Jake Hamon shooting and trial, followed by the breath of unspeakable corruption in high places in the Harding administration, then the sudden death of the president midway in his first term, followed by speculations of all sorts with hints of murder to cover up exposure and even suspicion toward Florence Harding.

The finale came with a long trial and imprisonment of several persons in highest offices of the government. Even my dad was subpoenaed to the hearings in Washington because of his luncheon with Jake Hamon at the convention in Chicago. They had only talked about the good old days in Oklahoma at the convention for statehood. They hadn't seen each other since those days. Hamon did give father the tip that Harding would be the next president.

I have about decided that there is no particular presidential timber. A candidate should be well educated, reasonably personable and attractive and with that added dash of charisma that helps him to get elected. He should be deeply concerned about the welfare of his country, not too one sided politically to be fair to those who disagree and not too deeply in the pockets of those who contribute to his campaign. It is pleasing to find that your president is an ideal family man, as president Bush seems to be. However, that hasn't always been essential to great leadership in world history.

Jake Hamon might well have been good presidential material for his organizational skills were super, he was a charmer personally, well educated, especially in law, a man of imagination certainly, and definitely an executive type. Also, he was a man of wealth who knew how to manage money. Evidently, he wasn't a womanizer as Harding and some others were, for he really loved Clara and, aside from his wife, there were no others. He definitely was expecting to run for president next time around and might well have made it. He might have been the better choice at the last convention

As to my references, the Jake Hamon story by Lone Quinby, was one of seven in the book, *"Murder for Love,"* published in 1931. I found it among my father's books and assume that he bought it because of Jake whom he knew quite well. The other stories all concerned women of the time who murdered for love, some pretty seamy stories. Also, I got some references on Harding from a new and interesting book by Richard Schenkman. It is called, *"Legends, Lies and Cherished Myths in American History"*.

And, I'll close with the final remark that, though we expect our presidents to be admired husbands and fathers, only in late years have we learned that many of our former presidents had most of the human flaws of the people they represented.

MY TRIBUTE TO GOLDEN

When our retirement years loomed ahead, the only thing we were sure of was that we wouldn't spend them in Chicago where we had had apartment living for the twenty-five years my husband had worked there.

Our two sons, a few years out or college, were married and the parents of small children. They had established homes in California and Colorado where we had visited them on long vacation trips to our country's glorious West. As it turned out, chance and good luck played a part in our settling in Golden. It began as an adventure and remained one.

Elder son, Douglas, had chosen to go to California to visit friends in the Malibu area. He decided to live in the region and to start his architectural practice there. He had done that and was off to a good start so wanted us to live nearby.

Younger son, David, was established in Golden, Colorado and chance had played a part in his arrival. Just out of college, he and a buddy decided to *"recuperate"* by taking a trip to Mexico City to visit friends taking summer courses at the university there. While there he was introduced to a fellow who was a teacher in the Denver public schools. When he learned that David would be looking for a teaching job, he offered to submit his name to the Jefferson County Board. He did that and after the exchange of several letters and a picture, David was hired to teach in Golden at Mitchel Elementary, the Junior High and a Golden Senior High. His subject was music.

Over the years we had visited my sister and family in Denver so had had trips to Golden, sight seeing drives through Clear Creek Canyon and many spectacular mountain areas that we loved. Those trips and many others were repeated when we visited Dave and family.

One happy day in Chicago we gave our landlord notice

that we would be leaving in a month, that was in April 1965. We had thirty days in which to find a home and to move.

Off we went on a drive to California. It was warm and lovely out there, too, and there was the ocean! We both loved to swim. We spent a delightful few days with Doug's family including the little girls, did a lot of driving on the crowded freeways and Doug even had a nice "spec" house he had designed and which was available to buy. He was very persuasive and all was very tempting except the freeways. We had a lot of that kind of driving around Chicago. But time was pushing us. We had to use some of it up on the drive back. We headed for Golden without deciding.

We even made a quick stop in the Walnut Creek area of Arizona and were favorably impressed by that region which would be about half way between our son's homes. But we hurried on.

Our Golden kids were very busy but took time to take us about on our search for a place to buy. I loved the mountains and we absorbed much of their beauty on our rounds. Secretly, I hoped to find a charming log cottage somewhere in them! There wasn't one and, since I am older, I have been eternally grateful!

Time was pushing from Chicago and our quest seemed to be quite a forlorn hope until we were just about ready to leave. Dave had news. He had learned that a cottage he and Ellyn once lived in was for sale. We had visited them there and knew the house, so he called the agent. He learned that someone else was considering it, but the deal was doubtful. That night his deal fell through and Dave called a lawyer friend. We all met along with the agent, papers were signed, money exchanged and we had a house! A modest, three-bedroom cottage with sizeable back yards big enough for a garden and there was a good view of the foothills and Castle Rock. The following morning found us furiously driving East to pack and to tie up dozens of odds and ends. We had only two weeks

Carpets went out for cleaning, furniture was sorted as we wanted to take only things that would be needed, books inherited from my dad had to be packed, too many, but I loved them all. I got busy packing them as I had so often as a girl when we were transferred, except now there was no time to browse as I did then!

Bundles of items went to Good Will and some were set-aside for relatives. We had a lot of help from those who lived in nearby suburbs. Finally all was ready and the movers came and the apartment where we had spent such a large portion of our lives was soon empty. Our last night was spent out in Glen Ellyn, Illinois with my sister and her family and we picked up my little mother who would live with us for a while. That was in May 1965.

After we were fairly well settled in Golden, Phil plowed up a sizeable area on one side of the yard for a garden and soon he planted that. The rest of the back yard grass was in poor condition but that would be sodded later.

At last order had been achieved and we were ready to start living our new life. We had time to become acquainted with our young grand children who already loved *"helping"* grandpa in the garden and who enjoyed accompanying us on many exploratory trips around town and in the mountains. We became friendly with the neighbors whose homes flanked ours on each side with Vina Ramstetter on the right and the Lee Suttons on the left.

Vina was a dear, quite elderly then, a former teacher for a great many years in the one-room schoolhouse in Golden Gate Canyon. It has since been preserved and brought down to grace the grounds of Mitchel Elementary School in Golden. Vina was a bright and most interesting lady who had lived a good part of Golden's history and entertained us with great stories. She made the wonderful old-fashioned Apple Dolls and dressed them in hand made lovely costumes. They often were displayed for the public. She was a reader and we often discussed books. Her own life would have made a good one as she, a graduate of Greely College, went as a teacher to live with a ranch family near Blackhawk, had fallen in love with one of the sons, married him and raised a family. We enjoyed and loved her.

On the other side lived the Suttons, much younger, parents of three boys, also most interesting for they had stories of the old days, too. The time came when Lee invited Phil to go on all-day fishing trips with him to the mountains. Phil loved to fish but had done all of his in Indiana lakes so it was an adventure for him to fish in our gorgeous mountains with a man who knew all of the good places and who taught him Colorado ways. The back yard seemed filled with fireflies the nights before each trip for they both were out there with flashlights snagging nosey worms to use for bait.

By summer time we were pretty well settled and beginning to enjoy retirement so looked forward to restful times. But, alas, that turned into a forlorn hope! The Illinois and Indiana relatives who had never been to Colorado, found us. Almost before we were fully settled the trek from the East began. These were people we loved, of course, and we took pleasure in showing off our lovely surroundings. We became glad that we had brought only sturdy furnishings and soon added a queen-sized sofa bed to the living room and bought a few cots. As summer progressed we seemed to have become something of a camp. There were times when some of the young ones slept rolled in blankets in the back yard!

My husband was the eldest of a family of eight, six boys and two girls and all of the sons were married as well as one sister. Each couple had two children except the sister. They had none. So I had seven sister in-laws and six brother in-laws. They were a close and loving family and every gathering of all was truly party time.

I used to say that I married into a League of Nations! The Rucker's had German and Norwegian backgrounds, one sister-in-law had a Hungarian dad, another was Polish on both sides and when I think of her I remember her wonderful Easter breakfasts at her home and my mouth waters for the delicious Polish sausage and home baked goodies. There always was an Easter egg hunt after dinner for the children. My own background added the British Isles with Scotch, Irish and English. We were all congenial and enjoyed being together. Some of the family lived in Chicago suburbia such as Elmwood Park where my Italian sister-in-law also served diet-busting delicious meals. Glen Ellyn, home of my only surviving sister was in distant Wauconda out in Lake country. Most of the others, including Phil's mother, lived in La Porte, Indiana. There was a lot of work with all of this entertaining, but our guests pitched in to help, also. Cooking wasn't such a problem for we often had cookouts or picnics. Sometimes the guests brought food and even cooked it. They helped hang out the wash, also, for the back yard was frequently decorated with sheets and other bedding. We had fun, too, as we labored! Of course there were endless sight seeing trips and the nearby mountains were the stars of the show.

We practically wore tracks to Lookout Mountain, Red Rocks, Clear Creek Canyon, Blackhawk, Central City, Estes Park, and Mt. Evans, even Boulder. All got a touch of nightlife on weekends when Dave and Ellyn played at the Robin's Nest on Lookout. They loved the exciting trip down Lariat Trail with the distant lights of Denver in view and those of Golden below.

So the happy retirement years sped by. We still were comfortable in the little cottage and still happy to have found it. It was great to have Dave and the grand children nearby and the young ones grew up almost too rapidly. Doug and family visited from time to time or we drove to California to see them. My mother enjoyed her life here, attended her church and had fun with her descendants. She died in 1973 at age 93. Her death was expected and she wanted to go. She was buried in Mt. Olivet Cemetery next to her daughter who once lived in Denver.

Much more of a shock in 1974 was Phil's sudden passing with a heart attack. We had watched the TV coverage of the Watergate scandal that caused President Nixon's resignation with great interest. On that night Phil said he felt tired, would shave and turn in. I finished watching the program and went to bed about ten thirty. He seemed to be asleep but was breathing strangely and noisily and that scared me. I called Dave and Ellyn who came at once. Phil heard the commotion and got up. He was at the bathroom door when he collapsed into David's arms. Dave gently placed him on the hall floor and began to give artificial respiration that he learned as a lifeguard. Ellyn called the doctor who called the rescue squad. They took him to the hospital and we followed, but his life was over!

I needed to be alone to come to grips with my emotions, so after my young folks took me home with them that night, I came back to build a new life in the little happy house that we had made a home. I lived as normal a life as was possible without drowning in tears and regrets. Phil had a most happy retirement of nine years, had fulfilled his dream of gardening and leisure at last for he had worked hard at his Chicago job, had been near his beloved sons, had loved playing with his grand children and watching them grow, never expressed regrets about our move, so I felt good about that. It was hard for me to reach our 50th anniversary alone when November 15th arrived. I must confess that I bawled pretty hard that day as such happy memories came flooding. But the result of that outburst was cleansing. I quit feeling sorry for myself and resolved to get along with living. The best part of my life was not yet over

Vina Ramstetter and Golden came to my rescue. Around that time she suggested that I drive her to a Garden Club meeting. I agreed, was a guest at the meeting and was invited to join. I met a lot of interesting women and was given a program book to peruse. I still have that book which was dated 1974-1975. Elizabeth Overstreet was president that year with Ilah Graaber, Vice President, Winnie Fletcher, Treasurer and Virginia Weigand, Secretary, as she still is. The monthly meetings were held at member's homes and began with a dessert lunch. That began an interesting phase for me, as members were such interesting and dedicated women. It was good to know them.

I got out into the city and began to realize that Golden was a progressive and wonderful place with a lot more than just history and beauty. Occasionally our meetings were held at Astor House, steeped in the past, but sometimes they were held in the Rec. Center with a whole modern atmosphere, busy with classes, meetings and with an outdoor popular swimming pool. The Club's focus was on the Annual Flower Show that it held in August. All worked very hard to put that on and most also exhibited flowers and other plants from their own gardens although the whole area brought their best. My interest has carried through to the present and some of the same women, now good friends, are still members as I am.

There was to be more socializing and Club work. In 1977, good friend and fellow Gardener, Marie Shier, took me to a meeting of the Delphian Study Club, started many years ago by women who wished to improve on their educations. Each member provided programs and they met twice monthly in the mornings from September until about May when the sessions ended with a fancy luncheon at some restaurant. Often the programs were on subjects that could be discussed by the members and some, as mine, were original essays, so I had a chance to write again. My dad who supported our family by writing as a newspaperman had programmed me at that. I had inherited his talent and he taught me a great deal and expected me to carry on.

My marriage at twenty-two took me away from the writing atmosphere. I really expected to get back into it at a later date but found it difficult to get my foot into the door then and also hard to find the solitude which writing demands. I was surrounded by young members of my husband's large and active family and was enough of a giddy girl then to enjoy the fun. We lived too close to them those first years when we returned from Florida with little money. Phil's mother gave him permission to turn a double garage on her property into a temporary apartment. But our fixing it up and making it into a studio is another story which I wrote at a later date and which was accepted by Better Homes and Gardens.

I found the Delphian's a most interesting group of women and am still a member. So another new and enriching life presented itself! In that same year there was to be another complete surprise. My much loved girl friend whom I met in Chicago as a new member of seventh grade, was Annitah, who took me under her wing and made me feel comfortable. We became life long friends and she still writes to me. She is an artist as is a daughter, Belle. They were to spend a couple of months in Europe and invited me to accompany them!

It seems that Belle's husband, a physics professor at Wisconsin U., was to spend two months teaching at Surry U. in England on summer grant. We flew to London, and while he attended meetings for two weeks in Warsaw, we would rent a car and drive across the Normandy area of France and take the train to Italy. We did that.

Belle spoke French well enough to get by and we really enjoyed the trip as we saw France at first hand by staying in bed and breakfast homes or small hotels, visiting ancient little churches as well as huge century-old cathedrals. We got caught up with a crowd of French women headed for mass in one of the chapels of Charte Cathedral and followed them to the pews where we sat and attended Mass with them. I happened to remember that date was June twenty-third so thought of my mother and dedicated my prayers to her! She would have been so pleased. It was my 75th birthday!

We all were history buffs and discussed that of William

the Conqueror who ruled the Norman territory we were traversing. What a beautiful part of France! We turned the car in at the Swiss border and took a fine train down to Florence, Italy. We had reservations at a four-story building which had been a fine home in the early centuries. It faced the Arno River and Bridge Trinita. It was in the old quarter so we walked our legs off visiting the studios of Michelangelo and the other greats. A glorious week followed by one in Rome where we went to the Vatican and Sistine Chapel and countless studios. We then took a plane back to England and were driven to Guildford, Surry, where Belle's husband would be teaching at Surry University.

The folks had sublet a house from a professor and family who would be spending their time in America, so it was as comfortable as our own homes. They rented a car again and we were in easy distances of many historic areas such as Stone Henge, Winchester Cathedral, etc. and spent many days reliving English history. We got to London a few times and even to Windsor Castle

In many ways Guildford reminded me of our Golden. To begin with, it had Gold in its name! A river ran through town instead of a creek. It had low, spacious and hilly downs instead of foothills, a college, as we do and was a pretty small city as ours is.

We were happy there and a bit reluctant to leave but finally the time arrived to fly home. Back in Golden, the accumulated mail brought another surprise. I found a letter from Tom Reynolds, a neighbor from my girlhood days in Lombard, Illinois. I had heard *about* him from time to time but not *from* him for a great many years. I knew that he was an engineer with degrees from Illinois and Columbia Universities, that he had worked for American oil companies abroad for a great many years in Saudi Arabia, Greece, Holland and Belgium, that his second marriage about fifteen years ago had been to a lovely Belgian widow of a music composer.

He had been a neighbor boy in Lombard and had played *"Cowboys and Indians"* with my brother down in the willow swamp that bordered our property. I was a few years older and loved to visit his writer mother, novelist Katharine Reynolds, who often gifted me with some of her *"fire-lit"* hours as she called them as we sat in rocking chairs beside her fireplace discussing authors, poetry, writing, etc. She also wrote short stories in manuscript form. She thought I had inherited the talents of my journalist father and was encouraging me. She and my parents were good friends as we all lived a good stone's throw from each other.

Tom's letter was a sad one. He had retired and had been in the midst of plans to return to America. He had hoped to buy a van and to take his wife on a year's tour of our beautiful country before settling down. She was a linguist who spoke six languages and had thought of possibly working part time as an interpreter. They had packed the things they wished to bring, given up the Brussels apartment, had their tickets to fly to New York, etc. She felt a little ill and decided to see her doctor who discovered a brain tumor and sent her to the hospital. She died eight days before they were scheduled to leave! Funeral services were held for her but a lonely and grieving Tom set out for his son's in Ohio bringing her ashes and her little dog, Regina.

His belongings were stored in an old farmhouse on property his son owned. All of this had been before he finally started to write letters. Through our letters to each other over a period of time we revived good Lombard memories and became acquainted as elders. Finally, since I lived alone and had spare rooms, I invited him to come for a visit. He accepted and came after Christmas with his Corvair loaded with books and classical recordings as well as the little dog, Regina. And, like *The Man Who Came to Dinner* stayed for nearly four years!

Tom was a complicated man as I soon learned. He was many faceted and it was impossible to know him on brief acquaintance. He met and liked my friends and neighbors. Many of them saw him as an outgoing sort who sang as he worked in the garden wearing a straw hat he had decorated with bright ribbons and laughed. He loved that. He was most interested in the Garden Club and couldn't understand why men couldn't belong. He did come down to lend a hand in setting up the Flower Show several times. He loved grocery shopping and talking to the ladies about recipes and such.

Tom was an avid planter of trees and everything he planted, grew. He loved roses and planted lots of them. They and the back yard garden flourished. One time he took some Alium seeds to the brook down the street and broadcast them along the banks among the weeds. The next year they bloomed. He made some birdhouses and put up a few feeders as he loved birds and could name them all.

But Tom had other sides for he was a perennial student and a voracious reader of books and had a passionate love for classical music. He had brought recordings by fine orchestras of the great masters and we often had our own concerts, which I also enjoyed. He was most interested in government and went to meetings at Mines or other places where governors or other representatives were speaking. He liked to meet them and even to correspond with some. He had a spiritual side but his knowledge of history and logic kept him guessing. As one might surmise, my life changed considerably but it was never dull!

Tom made trips back East from time to time to see members of his own family and finally faced up to his future and to the pain of unpacking the things Jannetje had so carefully packed. Finally he bought a house on acreage about six miles from his son in Canal Winchester, Ohio. Of course, be began planting trees! We corresponded regularly over the years but never saw each other again. He died in his sleep at age 84 last October. He did love Golden and it's people.

As to Golden, I'm still in love with it. Now, again, good

neighbors flank me. Boyd Barkey bought the Sutton house and keeps my garden plot planted so that I have home organically grown vegetables all summer. But he has been helpful in so many other ways, especially in my old age, that I call him my "middle son", since his age falls between those of my two sons. I've told him that he is the best Christian I know for he lives the part!

In Vina's house we have the young Nichols couple, Jill, who writes for the Golden Transcript and husband, Kevin, a county planner. So, intellectual pursuits still carry on.

I have learned to cope with old age by continuing to live from day to day without thinking too much about tomorrow, rather to think of the next day a clean slate with a possible pleasant surprise, and they happen surprisingly often!

One such day happened in late autumn when Marie and Ray Shier invited me to accompany them on a morning trip to see the aspens. We set out for Quinella Pass after a slow trip through Georgetown, a favorite with all. We chatted pleasantly for a while, but as we drove up into the scene of great splashes of gold above us and below us, we became quiet. It was a time of enchantment as we absorbed into our souls some of nature's miracles. We were practically alone for there were almost no other cars, and as we rose higher and higher the slim golden trees reached to the timber line with the darker, ragged peaks above topped by blue sky filled with soft white clouds. We truly experienced the rhythmic poetry of Nature and took home a day to remember.

At one of the Golden Garden's Club meetings, in 1977, I believe, the program was made up by members who each told of their early days in Golden, as the town was back then, school days, etc. It was interesting and fun. I had no such early days to recall, so wrote a poem to Golden as my contribution and read it. Virginia Weigand, then working on the Golden Transcript, had it published, but it came out while I was in Europe, and I would have missed it except that my daughter-in-law saved some copies. I think it is fitting for an end to my saga of Golden, so will finish with that.

To Golden

When retirement years proclaimed the time,
We longed to flee from the rush of the city
On the sprawling prairie we called home.
We had visions of mountains and canyons and streams
And a jewel of a city, in such a setting,
A place to retire but not to stagnate,
A yard for a garden and flowers and trees.
So, following loved ones, who had come before,
We found Golden with an open door,
And a modest cottage with a view all around
Of foothills rising to mountain peaks
Slashed by waters of tumbling creeks
And raggedly framing the bluest sky!
With access roads in all directions
To lovely lakes with cloud reflections.
So we came and stayed and loved it here
And learned that Golden has so much more
In the kind of people of whom one dreams
Who are warm and friendly and filled, it seems,
With tales of the regions exciting past;
With ancestral ghosts who live among them.
We loved their stories of mining days
And those of the rancher's and gardeners' phase.
So, we discovered our jewel in a Golden setting
With plenty of schools, with music and art
And a college of Mines of world renown;
With a brewery, too, very much a part!
We found churches and shops and civic pride
And even a newspaper to keep us in stride.
But his saga of Golden becomes too long.
It can't be chanted in just one song.

FLORIDA BOUND VAGABONDS

It seemed like a crazy off the cuff suggestion that lovely summer Sunday afternoon. My newly married sister, Marguerite, was telling of plans for herself and young husband, Bill Kennard, to quit their jobs in the Chicago area and head for Florida in the autumn. They hadn't gone on a honeymoon and felt that they deserved one. They were living temporarily in our family home in Lombard, Illinois and thought that it was time to start out on their own.

Phil Rucker, my guest, was with us as we lounged on the tree shaded side lawn, chatting. Bill had spent a number of winters in Florida with his parents as a lad and had fond memories of swimming, fishing and boating in that delightful climate while the North was in a deep freeze. We others had never been there.

The more I listened the better it sounded. Perhaps I could defer my dream of living on the left bank of the Seine in Paris and becoming the writer that my talents indicated. As children, Marguerite and I had always made adventures of traveling together as we moved about with a transferred journalist father and I wasn't sure that I liked the idea of her going without me!

Phil and I worked for the same company in Maywood and had dated from time to time but no word of romance had ever passed between us. We were good friends and he had such a delightful sense of humor that we always laughed a great deal together. He also loved dancing as I did and was a great escort to Chicago's palatial ballrooms. Finally, I exclaimed, *"Oh. I want to go along!"* Their answer was, *"Fine! Bring Phil and come along!"* Of course, none of us really meant that then.

However, the seed had been planted and before long it began to sprout. Phil was the oldest at age twenty-five. He worked in the field of sheet metal advertising as a model maker and mentioned that he hadn't had a vacation in several years. He began to convince himself that one was due. I was twenty-two and lived with my parents so had no financial obligations. Bill was twenty-two, also, and Marguerite would be twenty-one in September. They were anxious to get on with married life.

Our youth and immaturity was evident as adventure beckoned. Soon we were talking as if a foursome would be great fun and the fact that we could share expenses was most attractive as none of us had much money.

Before too many days went by we decided to do it! October first was targeted as starting date. As it turned out, preparations for the trip provided an exciting and rewarding project for the summer.

The boys bought an old Model T Ford for a reasonable sum and we all began to plan equipment. A great deal of creativity went into this, as we had to hold supplies to a minimum. We devised a cabinet just wide enough to rest on the left of the running board and as high as the door tops. It was built of lightweight wood and equipped with numerous shelves for specific items such as spices, sugar, flour, eggs, cereal, etc. The bottom area had a place for a two-burner gasoline stove, water container, coffee pot, dishes and such. The cabinet was screwed to the running board and could be easily removed. Its door was hinged at the bottom with fastening at top center. All necessary items would be disclosed when we lowered it to become our table.

Phil's cousin, Wallace Stalker, provided an old tent that was cut in two so that half could be fastened on the top of the car and it would open to the left side. The cabinet would be enclosed when the tent was staked down.

Two thin couch mattresses were purchased and placed side by side on the canvas tent floor for sleeping four people; their lengths became the bed width. For travel they could be stacked on top of the car and covered by the neatly folded tent. The original Model T Ford had no trunks so a rack was built on the front bumper to carry our meager luggage. We took only clothing needed for the trip and would send for trunks later if we decided to stay.

Blankets were folded and placed on car seats and anything else would have to ride inside with us. All decided to wear flannel shirts and knickers with wool socks for travel and high boots for the boys. These were daring costumes for Marguerite and me in that day of rather long skirts but we wanted to be trendsetters. All brought changes and one dress-up outfit.

Bill Kennard sitting by traveling car.

Finally, all was ready and autumn was approaching. Phil's mother had invited us all to Sunday dinner in her Chicago home and we had met all of his large family. He and I had become much better friends, but only that, in spite of what our relatives and friends thought. I had no scruples about going on a trip with him and couldn't understand why anyone would question it. My parents trusted me. Phil's brother, Bud, drove him from work to our house the night before we were to leave. He stayed for supper and left early. At bedtime Marg and I exchanged good-byes with young brothers, John and Paul, and sister, Helen, as we planned to leave at five in the morning. Father and I traded typewriters so that I could take his portable. My plan was to keep a daily journal of our progress and I promised to send several copies at a time to him and Mother. They would relay them to the families of Bill and Phil.

We awoke on October first to find a clear sky and a perfectly gorgeous frosty dawn. Our parents were up and breakfast was ready. It was consumed hurriedly as excitement was mounting. There were hugs and kisses for Marg and me and warm handshakes for our companions. I did hear Father say in a quiet voice to Bill, *"She's in your care and I appoint you her chaperone."* As we pulled out of the drive waving, Marg and I observed two smiling but concerned parents waving back.

Light hearted and absolutely carefree we probably were happier then than we ever would be again. Bill was driving with Marg beside him as he steered our strange looking vehicle through Lombard toward Chicago and the Outer Drive, which skirted Lake Michigan on its way to Indiana. In those early days for cars, Fords were nicknamed Tin Lizzies and we began to refer to our traveling home, unoriginally, as Lizzie or Liz.

The weather grew progressively more glorious as the sun arose over the great lake and the early frost vanished. The roads were good and the car perked along at about thirty miles an hour. We chatted and laughed and even sang a song that became our theme, the popular, *Let the Rest of the World Go By*.

Marg and Bill had been married since the previous November. Neither had dated any other since they were in their teens. Bill was a movie star handsome lad and Marguerite, very pretty in the Irish Colleen tradition, and they had been voted the best looking young couple in town. They had eloped but I was let in on the affair the night before so I accompanied them to the judge in Wheaton, the County seat.

We arrived in South Bend, Indiana before noon and walked about town to stretch our legs. To his great surprise, Phil ran into his cousin, Auburn, and her husband, Bob. They would relay the fact that the travelers were on their way.

After lunch we changed drivers and Phil took over while I sat beside him in front. Marg and I hadn't learned to drive as not many women did in those early days of motorcars.

Bill and Marguerite Kennard, Phil Rucker, Eva Costello

Each had specific chores and we established a routine that became automatic as the days accumulated.

That first morning Marg and I made pancakes for breakfast with bacon and coffee while the boys took up the bedding and placed it atop the car. We had arisen at six and while we girls washed up in a nearby stream, they made a small bonfire. Then they washed up and came back to camp. We sat on the tent floor with two at the center of the lowered door and one on each end. All were ready to welcome the new day, another beauty, and the teasing and kidding seldom stopped. Phil picked up one of the pan-sized pancakes and, stepping outside, sailed it into the air like a discus. The two clowns kept asking if we had any more rubber blankets, but they did eat them.

We headed east about eight o'clock that morning. I placed the typewriter on my lap and began recording our adventures as the wind ruffled the pages so that I could hardly see them at times. The Liz was wide open, as it was the side curtain vintage and they were rolled up on good days. Our first stop was in town for post cards, stamps and candy.

Then on to Toledo and Venice, Ohio, where we stopped for a walk beside Sandusky Bay, picking up shells for souvenirs and enjoying the scenery. We had no particular time schedule so decided to camp for the night in a field overlooking Lake Erie. Had early supper as all were tired and turned in early.

The third day was a great one as all had slept deeply and felt refreshed. Our route took us through Lorraine where we viewed the devastation of the recent tornado. There were many wrecked homes although rebuilding had begun. The highway hugged the shore of Lake Erie and led us to Cleveland. None had ever seen such a collection of costly mansions and the beauty of the city impressed estates and us even after we left that area to buy the day's supplies.

Bill drove the morning shift and Phil took over in the

afternoons. The beauties of Pennsylvania awaited us as the terrain became hillier and we began to notice the brilliantly colored leaves on roadside trees. We began to look for a camp beyond North East and found one there. Had a hot supper and will quote from the diary. *"This is the life! Dishes are washed and as I write, Marg is doing her postcards and the boys are singing to the accompaniment of Bill's ukulele, harmonizing so that I can hardly concentrate. We are about two miles from the New York State Line."*

Buffalo is seventy-five miles away and we are five hundred twenty-five miles away from home. We bought supplies in town and drove on through for we were anxious to see Niagara Falls. When we arrived we where excited for they were spectacular beyond our ability to describe or to have imagined them. Were surprised to find almost no one else around, so parked the Liz and asked an elderly policeman if he would keep an eye on it while we investigated. He said, *"Sure."*

We found a shaft that contained an elevator and a descending stairway. It would cost a nickel apiece to ride down so we laughed and chose to walk down the twenty-three flights! Strolled about on the rocks below some twenty feet from the falls and it was sheer delight to look and to listen to the roar and to feel the spray all about us. We were quite damp when we finally decided to ride the elevator to the top for the huge twenty-cent fee for all.

We found the old Irish policeman sitting on the edge of the bumper and asked him if he'd mind doing it once more. He grinned and waved us on. We hiked across the long bridge that led to Canada after paying the ten-cent toll. Looking back from the other side we agreed that we thought the Canadian views were even more stunning than those from the American side.

Niagara Falls

We climbed down to the water's edge near the Maid of the Mist landing. Before leaving Canada we treated ourselves to a delicious sundae at the Queen's Restaurant. Our policeman had left by the time we returned but old Liz was intact. We drove through Goat Island and decided that the rapids were almost as thrilling as the Falls themselves.

Then it was time to leave to find a camp, hopefully, before dark. It was raining hard by the time we pitched the tent in a woodsy spot a couple of miles from the Falls. Fires were not allowed so we ate a cold supper. Exhausted as we felt, we indulged in a short songfest before turning in to be lulled to sleep by the distant roar of Niagara Falls.

The next day, October fifth, was our first Sunday on the road. It was still raining so we backtracked to Buffalo where we treated ourselves to a very good meal for thirty-five cents each. We lost our trail in town and circled around Buffalo asking questions of pedestrians. Everyone gave us a different answer and with Phil's delightful mimicry we got to laughing so hard it became a game. We finally discovered the trail ourselves and spent several hours driving through charming little New York towns.

It was about mid-afternoon when we came upon a pretty camping spot and put up for the rest of the day to enjoy an area of colorful trees and a splendid view of the countryside. Had early supper and washed the dishes while the boys chatted with several farmers who came out of curiosity but were nice friendly fellows. My notes for the day ended with, *"While I write, Marguerite is rinsing dish towels, Phil is peeling and cutting apples for apple sauce and Bill is tending fire and playing ukulele by turns. "*

And so we traveled on utterly happy and carefree. The elegant Alleghenies, resplendent in their autumn colors, left Marg and me almost speechless with delight. We had never seen mountains before and certainly none so gorgeously attired so that we kept exclaiming, *"Look! Oh, look!"*

Bill had seen these and the Cumberland's and others and Phil had spent one summer in the Rockies area so they teased us by saying that these were mere hills. Wonderful paved roads ran in and out through the valleys for a time and then began to wind up and up. Towns seemed scarce and we saw only a few houses, quite elegant ones.

At one point we all were so thrilled by our gorgeous surroundings that we simply had to become part of them. Old Liz was parked at roadside and we got out and walked about, even drank water that bubbled over rocks at roadside.

Farther along we found a nice camp with two gas ranges served by natural gas. Pitched the tent on the banks of the Susquehanna River in the shadow of a mountain and slept that night lulled by the music of rapid river waters.

Next morning we continued along the Susquehanna Trail to Harrisburg and encountered our first toll bridges, three of them. The fee for the first one was ten cents, the second, a quarter and the third only a nickel and we all agreed that it was the best one. There were to be other toll bridges and we had a laugh at Phil who would make a comical remark and flip a coin into the river where we crossed a bridge without a toll.

Gettysburg was our next destination and our tour there was most interesting and moving for we saw the monuments of ferocious fighting in the Civil War battles. We learned some of the gory details and visited the home of Jenny Wade where we were told her story, as she was the only civilian killed in the battle. A bullet went through two doors and struck her as she was mixing dough in the kitchen. She had come to be with her sister to help care for her newborn baby. We were told that the sister still lives at age 86 and that the baby is now a grandfather.

October eighth was not very jolly as we had planned an early start but had gone only sixty-two miles when Bill pulled to the side of the road. Transmission bands had worn out from constant use of brakes in the hills. Phil had hitched a ride to a service station where he bought the bands for a dollar twenty and we put up for three hours while the boys did the work on them.

Evelyn kneeling by river.

Florida Bound Vagabonds

After buying groceries, we drove on to Washington, D.C. There was no time then for sight seeing so we located a tourist camp on an island in the Potomac near the Washington Monument. It was the largest camp but not the best we had seen. It was swarming with tourists and we learned that most of them were Florida bound. Supper was soon prepared and we were hungry for we had missed lunch. After dark it was most interesting to see the brilliant lights on the Capitol dome. Sleep came early.

Next morning, at exactly nine o'clock, opening time, we were at Washington Monument ready to go to the top with the first party. The shaft is five hundred feet high and the view from the top truly spectacular. Much of the city was visible as the streets extend out from the center as the spokes from a wheel. We had a good look at Calvin Coolidge's White House, the Capitol Building, the hub so to speak, Robert E. Lee's home and many others.

Naturally, we were the only ones to walk down the seemingly endless flights of stairs! Before long we were with a group to tour the Capitol with a guide who pointed out the various chambers of government and answered questions. We left there hoping to go to the White House but had missed the morning tour so decided to drive around it and gaze at the executive mansion's imposing exterior. Then we got under way and soon entered Virginia.

It wasn't long before we realized that we had left fine roads behind us. There were long stretches of hard bottom gravel roads of brick color and many hills to climb. The dust and color were hard on Phil's eyes as he was the pilot. The front left wheel struck a sharp rock and we had our first puncture. Quote from the journal: *"...however, we still are enthusiastic about traveling and have found it very inexpensive so far. We have spent $14.85 on gas and oil and $28.33 on provisions and other expenses including tolls, camp fees, cards, etc. Less than twelve dollars apiece and we have traveled twelve hundred and fifty miles! Gas* *prices have ranged from sixteen to twenty cents a gallon."*

All of the next day was spent on Virginia's rather bad roads, but we really enjoyed the picturesque countryside. We also had more punctures with the ailing two tires. The boys patched inner tubes at roadside quite expertly.

Shortly before sundown we camped at Middleburg, North Carolina, a tiny town that seemed populated mainly by blacks. We found ourselves in a lonely churchyard but no one bothered us and we cooked a good supper. Also enjoyed a moonlit and restful evening.

We were up early the next morning but took the time to have a leisurely breakfast. Then washed the dishes, packed and hit the road by eight. Found the roads getting worse as they were composed of red clay or clay and sand mixture or gravel with little glass particles. They were pretty hard on tires and second hand Lizzies. We pulled off by a stream and walked about. Phil and I dunked our heads in the river and washed our hair to the tune of laughter from Marg and Bill.

Phil and Eva relaxing in the river

Cotton plantations now became our chief scenery. The plants were heavy with blooms, white and seemingly ready for picking. Towns were far apart and most were made up of shacks and a few shabby stores. It was difficult to find a place that night, as there were no camps. We reached the town of Ellerbe and once again put up in an old tumbledown churchyard. No one bothered us so the boys made a fire of dry pine tree branches and needles. We had driven a hundred and sixty miles and felt that that would be about the best we could do for the rest of the trip. The night was gorgeous again in bright moonlight.

We had seen the slogan, and since the roads were becoming progressively worse, decided to enjoy the sky at least. Other tourists had told us that the ones in Georgia and Florida were as bad or even worse.

Sunday was our twelfth day out and we decided to make it an easy one by driving until noon, making a good dinner and just loafing. Fate made another decision.

At ten A.M., when we had traveled about fourteen miles, a connecting rod bearing burned out! We were four miles from the nearest town so once again Phil hailed a lift from a passing car. We had a long wait until he returned with the necessary parts. Once again the boys did the work and our two good mechanics had old Lizzie purring better than when we started. Marguerite and I congratulated ourselves *(and them)* that we accompanied men of such talents. We left at three o'clock.

At Cheraw, South Carolina, we bought delicious dinners that consisted of southern fried chicken, rice, potatoes, soup and ice cream all for sixty cents each. About three miles past Cheraw we came upon a dandy camp and put up for the night. Pitched the tent in the woods beside a swift little stream. While Marguerite washed towels in the stream, the boys discovered a swimming pool nearby. It was marked Private but we got into our suits and had good workouts, as the water was cold. All felt cleansed and invigorated afterwards.

At dark we all were sitting out by a campfire, singing and eating candy when two old timers and three young men came to visit. They were curious, polite and friendly and told us stories about the area. We really enjoyed them but were ready for a really good sleep when they left.

We were awakened around five the next morning by the singing of darkies, cotton pickers as they went to work. Later, just before breakfast, Marguerite and I saw a Ford come tearing along the road, strike a big hole and roll over completely! The boys had been back in the woods so we called to them frantically and as they ran toward the car, we saw Negro men crawling from under the wreck. Five came out, seemingly unhurt, for they started to run away. The boys called them back fiercely to help lift the car off two others who were pinned down. One got up and could walk. He was the driver and car owner. The other lay on the ground, stunned at first, and then he started rolling and moaning. He clung to Phil and kept crying, over and over, *"Oh, Lawd, tell me I ain't guine die."* Phil tried to assure him that he wasn't and helped to lift him into the first car that came along to take him to the hospital. All of the men were picked up as other cars arrived.

We fixed breakfast after the excitement and got off to a late start. Bill kidded Phil about being mistaken for the "Lawd" by the poor injured man but we all hoped that he wasn't too badly hurt.

The day took us through Camden and Columbia, South Carolina and at night we camped in the large front yard of some farmers. They called their place, which is new, *Hill of View Camp Site*. After we had eaten Bill brought out his "*uke*" and began to strum it. Upon hearing the music, a Mr. De Bose came out and invited us inside his home. Others were there, including a lady who introduced herself as a music teacher from Pennsylvania and she played the piano for us. Then Mr. De Bose asked for a song from us. We sang our theme that had been pretty well rehearsed by this time. Mr. De Bose then played his violin and mouth organ and we danced. It turned into a fun party evening and we stayed up later than at any time on the trip. Two girls, Thelma and Addie May, asked us to send them a card from Jacksonville as they became quite friendly.

Marg, Phil, Eva, and Bill as Phil pumps and Eva holds.

    The next morning we found that the oatmeal we had set to soak was gone. The lid had been knocked off the pan and we assumed that we had had a dog visitor during the night. When I went to get the bacon, it and the lunchmeat were missing, also. The dog again, we felt sure. He must have been busy while we were in the house. We laughed about that but it wasn't so funny to discover that nearly a pound of butter and a bag of sugar also had vanished. Darn funny dog that would eat all of that stuff and the paper containers as well!

We left, bought groceries in Augusta, and hurried on through. The scenery grew interesting, as much of it was swampland. We saw our first palmetto palms, today. Also, that gray green hanging Spanish Moss intrigued me. It seems to have no roots and to thrive on air and tree bark. We drove to Metter, Georgia, about a hundred thirty miles and camped behind the Court House and across from the Fair Grounds. Found ourselves beside some folks bound for Jacksonville. Made a good supper composed of pork chops, sweet potatoes and pineapple.

Phil and I strolled over to the Fair Grounds, afterwards, and around them to discover a medicine show in progress. Phil was more thoughtful than I was about giving the young marrieds some private time.

From the diary; *"We weren't in a hurry to leave this morning as we have planned to take two days to drive to Jacksonville. It is one hundred sixty-one miles away. None is paved and recently heavy rains have torn up some of them, as they seem to cut through swampy, moss-draped pine forests. There are many bridges and some look undercut and wobbly. We felt a fairy tale eeriness about the trip to Waycross but we arrived without incident."*

The campground there was crowded with travelers, the greatest collection we have seen thus far, and all bound for one place. There were many men with families along, all seemingly on a shoestring and with no certain prospects of work.

The large campground cost a quarter admission and we had the use of decent kitchen and bathroom facilities. I would have enjoyed it except for the menagerie arranged about its edges. There were monkeys, two owls, squirrels, a skunk, alligators and various types of snakes.

We still were a happy and care free foursome but that evening brought us back to reality as we talked with some of our neighbors. The family right next to us had been on the road for two years and had logged thirty-seven thousand miles. An elderly blind relative helped to support them by *canvassing* but we felt sure that meant begging.

A medicine Show man came to see us when he heard us singing to Bill's accompaniment on his ukulele. He was seeking professionals to travel with him as demonstrators.

A little Ohio girl spent most of the evening sitting beside our tent. She said we were the happiest people she had seen for a long time. We went to bed with more sober thoughts that night.

It was about ten-thirty the following morning when we finally started and shortly before noon we reached the infamous corduroy road which all had warned us about. It was a detour some twenty miles long and Phil commented that it was at least forty miles up and down as there would be a stretch of cross wise logs and sand fill, then another of sand and clay, followed by another area of logs. We crept along as slowly as possible, while the car jounced up and down and side ways as we cut right through a pine forest. There were only a very few dwellings.

We seemed to travel in half-light as the pines screened out the sun. We were about half way when we saw a small house. We asked if we might park in the front and received permission from the lady who also sold us some persimmons. These were about the size of an orange and nearly the same color and were strange fruits to us. They had a bland, mealy texture and we would need to cultivate a taste for them we decided unanimously. We also had our first taste of sculpture flavored water which smelled at first like sewer gas which sometimes came up from our basement back home. Later we learned that after it had been allowed to set for a while after it had been drawn it lost its odor and that, chilled, it was quite as good as well as healthy.

Phil and Bill laughing.

It seemed forever, but we finally reached Jacksonville where we found a very good camp. We turned in rather early that night after attempting to form a plan of action.

Tuesday, October 21, 1924
The boys will make the first attempt to find jobs. They will canvas Jacksonville and, if unsuccessful, we'll move on. Marg and I intend to try, too, but only after they find employment because we all must stay together.

The town is swarming with tourists, mostly men, but

some have wives and children along. We still aren't worried, as we have learned that we can live frugally, if necessary.

Bill and Phil changed into their rather wrinkled best clothes and set out on the nearby trolley. Marg and I borrowed a tub and washboard from the camper next to us, scrubbed all of our soiled clothes and hung them out on her line. Then we gave the tent and car a good cleaning. The day was really beautiful and we were camped in the center of a pine forest. The place was well kept with clean facilities and it would cost only a dollar for a week's stay. We were surrounded by tourists so wouldn't want for conversation. The boys returned late in the afternoon without jobs.

They tried again for several days and it seemed quite hopeless. On Sunday we decided to drive to Pablo Beach and had our first swim in the Atlantic Ocean. The day was gray and the waves rolled high but the water was warm and we plunged in with delight. Found that swimming was harder than in a pool but diving through the waves was something new and great fun. We were reluctant to return to camp, made it as late as possible and had dinner well after dark.

Monday morning began a day's change of pace. We got up early so that the boys could begin the search. Marg and I did our house chores, gossiped some with our little Tennessee neighbor lady, then decided to dress and go to town. Hauled out our civilized costumes, putting dresses on for the first time in three weeks. They felt good, too!

Then we walked about three blocks to the trolley and paid a nickel apiece for the ride to town. Got off in the heart of Jacksonville and strolled about to become oriented. At Cohen's Department Store we each bought an apron. Kept looking for ads for workers and asked questions of sales- people. Neither had had any practice in job hunting and, had we found one, may not have taken it, for the first employment would depend on the boys.

I probably was more concerned about work because I had promised my parents to at least save enough for train fare home. Marg could live on Bill's wages, but, of course, I would have to pay my own way. Anything else was just not done in that day.

We had a good lunch at the Wisteria Candy Shop, a tasty full meal for fifty cents apiece. Then we took in a movie at the Imperial and enjoyed Bebe Daniels in *Dangerous Money*. It was most pleasant to walk about the city and we agreed that we could easily like Jacksonville as we headed for the streetcar.

We were about half way back to Camp when we looked out the window and saw old Lizzie parked near the car line as the two men watched for us! They had returned from their search without results, planning to take us to the beach and had read Marg's note. Now we have decided to head for Tampa, tomorrow.

The sisters, Evelyn and Marguerite, by the river.

Florida Bound Vagabonds

We rather regretfully broke down camp after our five day sojourn, we had become friendly with the Tennessee woman and had pleasant chats with a couple of rather queer old fellows, brothers, who camped nearby. One spent much time gathering long pine needles as he wove baskets and the other hardly moved but seemed to sit all day reading his paper.

We were on the road by ten o'clock and then, whoops! A flat tire! It was rim cut and we bought a new one for eleven dollars. We put up at four at Columbus Springs Camp that was nicely equipped and even had a small lake with springboard and water slide. There also was a small dance pavilion with an electric piano as well as the usual toilet facilities and good drinking water. Marg and I wanted to go swimming but our boys got a bit bossy and said the water was too cold. It did look cold with lots of little springs bubbling up. It was hard to believe that we had it all to ourselves.

Wednesday, October 22nd, 1924

Phil's 26th birthday, we gave Phil his 26 spanking first thing this morning. His only other gift was an Italian Brier pipe I had bought in hope that he would quit smoking cigarettes. He used Camels while Bill smoked Lucky Strikes. (Marg and I didn't acquire that bad habit until many years later.) We made a hearty breakfast and didn't leave until about ten o'clock. Then we had to take a roundabout route to Tampa because of bad roads.

Cars were comparatively new yet in 1924 and America was just getting around to making the highways to accommodate them. We had covered about a hundred miles when we struck a fine camp at Inverness. It was only four o'clock but we decided to stay as the days were getting shorter and we didn't like making supper after dark. Marguerite and I had set our watches to Eastern Time but, to tease us, Bill and Phil insisted that they had the right time that was an hour earlier.

I should mention here that we all got along together very

well. There had been no real arguments or crosswords. Naturally, there was plenty of teasing banter when they took sides against us or we against them, but only in fun and all knew that.

Propinquity had played its part and Phil and I were much more affectionate with each other. But first we were very good friends who seemed to understand and enjoy each other. Not that we were very much alike for we couldn't have been more different. Perhaps that very fact made each more interesting to the other. Physical attraction was there as well.

Thursday, October 23rd, 1924

Sun shone brightly this morning but hardly penetrated the thick grove we were in. Marguerite and I wanted to get started early but the boys had the fishing bug so it was past ten-thirty when we gave up and spent the rest of the day there. A few fish struck but none hung on. We gals did enjoy our stay for we got into our swimsuits and found that the water was much warmer than the air. We had early supper and Phil and I walked to town to see a movie. It was Grandmother's Boy starring Harold Lloyd and we loved it. Plan is to head for Tampa tomorrow. It is only eight miles away.

Friday, October 24, 1924

Arrived in Tampa before noon and finally found Six Mile Camp and set up our tent. It was an excellent camp with all facilities such as running water, showers, cooking facilities, etc., and only twenty-five cents a night or a dollar a week. We paid the dollar. The only flaw is that we are about two miles from the trolley line so the boys will have to take the Lizzie to look for work.

Saturday was spent at camp, hiking along the creek, meeting fellow travelers, and generally amusing us. We enjoyed a Kentucky couple and learned a lot about economic conditions from them. They had come to pick fruit in Orlando but now were anxious to return to their Kentucky hills. After supper we watched a show on the campgrounds as part of a crowd. A man who billed himself as a world famous human spider performed clever stunts with ropes and finished by climbing a rope ladder claiming that only he, and perhaps a few others, could accomplish that. He passed his hat afterward and announced that his take was four dollars. Then his young helper wiggled out of a straight jacket and passed his hat. They challenged anyone who wished to try to climb the ladder. Phil and Bill tried and failed but Bill got a hand for his good effort and a laugh when he removed his hat as if to pass it.

On Sunday we took a trip to Clearwater that was reached by a very long bridge as it was on a peninsula. Had our first delightful swim in the Gulf of Mexico and loved it as the water was warm and seemed so clean. Winter tourists had not yet begun to arrive and, since we were practically alone, we tried all of the wonderful beach playthings such as swings, merry-go-round, rings, etc. We spent many hours there, forgetting about our over-exposure to the sun, to our later regret.

Old Liz had developed a knock, which baffled the boys, so on Monday they tore down the engine while Marg and I washed and dried some things, and generally prepared for departure next day for Oldsmar. The boys worked hard and it was suppertime when they had the engine back together, with the knock still in it!

We did start for Oldsmar next morning but never arrived there for the boys stopped first at an employment agency and found jobs as roofer helpers!

Instead, we moved to Sulphur Springs just outside of Tampa to the back yard of their future boss. Consulting the diary, I find the following: *"Now we are situated at the top of a sand hill at the far back end of the lot. There is a pump nearby and an outhouse is available. Fred Rousch, his wife and three young children, as well as his mother-in-law, live in the rather large house at the front. They have been nice* to us and we like them.

There are bushes and trees on one side and they screen us from our next-door neighbor who runs a clean little general store. He has told us that he is a New Jersey Jew with a Polish wife and they gave us some boxes upon which to place a gasoline stove bought this morning from some campers who charged only five dollars. We arranged to walk about two blocks to check out the Sulphur Springs pool that was advertised as *"The Fountain of Youth Makes the Old Young and the Young, Younger."*

It is a very large circular pool and seems to be fed by springs. It has a water slide outlet into a stream that eventually becomes the home of alligators, part of an adjacent farm for them. A park that also houses a stand for music and dancing surrounds the pool.

Marg and Bill on diving platform.

We learned that there was a sixty-five cent fee if one rented a suit there, thirty-five cents for bringing your own and only ten if you came wearing your suit. We paid the dime a piece and dived into the water that was said to register seventy- two degrees the year around. All were delighted to find this wonderful place near-by.

On Wednesday, October 29th, we all piled out at five-thirty to cook a good breakfast for the boys and were waiting for Fred Rousch long before it was time to leave at a quarter of seven.

Marg and I got all of our clothes ready for washing, borrowed a tub from Mrs. Rousch and bought a washboard and some apron material from the general store next door. I cut out and made aprons for Marg and me while she washed. We are so tired of wearing knickers. Bought more goods and made us each an underskirt as well. Then started to fix supper. We had a really busy day.

Our workmen arrived home at six and such forlorn creatures we couldn't have imagined! They had posed as being experienced roofers that they were not. Phil had roofed a garage at home, but Bill was a complete novice. The day had been very hard on their clothing as well, for the seats of their britches were worn and their socks were rags - almost off their feet! They had bought overhauls and would get tennis shoes. They plan to look for other work but will stay with this as long as the boss allows. The pay is $24.00 a week that is pretty good considering Florida wage scales.

They felt much better after washing up, changing clothes and eating a good meal. Then we all had good laughs at their descriptions of their day. They hadn't minded the work that they said was healthy and already both had becoming tans.

After our men left the next morning and we had tidied up, we were wondering how we would fill the day. It was then that Mrs. Rousch invited us to accompany her to the grapefruit-packing house that was about a mile away. It was most interesting and we saw how the fruit is washed, dried, sorted and packed for shipment.

I should interject, here, that Father had written urging me to try to write some articles on just such a visit, so I talked to one of the men until their boss came in. He began to tell us all about the place. It seems the *"regulars"*, as he called them, do nothing else but pack fruits, traveling from state to state, town to town.

Phil and Bill in good humor.

The regulars were still in Georgia doing peaches and the ones we saw today just filled in as odd hands picked to do the earliest fruit. The other would be in next week to start grapefruit and oranges. He told us to take as many culls as we could eat and he explained that *"culls"* were fruit which had gone through the process, but in sorting, were either too big, too small or too ripe, so had been thrown aside. We helped ourselves to all we could carry and later found that all were delicious. Mrs. Rousch said that the best ones would come in January.

The boys were not so discouraged when they arrived home that evening. Neither had gone through his overhauls and both wore new tennis shoes. We had had a good laugh at them that morning when both discovered that they had only silk socks to wear after ruining the wool ones. We brought out some of our cotton socks and Phil quickly put a pair of mine on, but Bill balked at wearing a girl's socks. However, he finally and reluctantly did so.

There was little for us gals to do that day so we decided to take the nickel ride to Tampa on the trolley. We checked the Post Office for mail and found welcome letters from home. We entered a nice department store, browsed some, as well as inquiring about openings for sales persons. No one needed. Then we found the rest lounge and sat comfortably reading our letters. We thought of seeing a movie but found nothing of interest, so returned to Sulphur Springs.

The boys came back in a cheerier mood that night, confident that they would soon be experienced roofers. They worked only half a day on Saturday as they had finished one house and Fred didn't want to start another, as they always took a half-day off.

We couples scattered to pursue different interests, but first, all went for a swim at the Fountain of Youth after which we had lunch. Then Marg and Bill took off for the alligator farm which they really enjoyed while Phil and I went with Fred's brothers, Dave, aged 17 and Burt, aged 20, *(both apprentice roofers and great bunk artists, but most amusing)* to the fruit packing house in their truck. Oranges were being packed that day, but we came back with gunnysacks filled with a hundred culls each of grapefruit for a dollar a bag. That night Phil and I dressed up and went back to the park to listen to the good music and to dance. November first was to become memorable. The dance pavilion was colorfully lighted and we whirled through a fox trot and a waltz before strolling outside where the lights, filtered through Spanish moss covered trees, were eerie and romantic. We moved slowly down toward the bank of the Hillsboro River and found a bench in the twilight. The melodic numbers of the orchestra had us swaying even as we sat. However, I was about to have an interesting discussion. My funds were running low and I had promised my parents to save enough for train fare home in that case. Marg could live off the wages of her husband, but I would either have to support myself or go home. That would have to be soon unless I could find work, which didn't seem likely. Phil sat quietly for a few minutes and then he did a touching thing.

Phil and Eva with the alligator.

Bill and Marg, with the alligator.

He slipped down to one knee and, taking my hand, said, *"We could get married, couldn't we?"* With the embraces and kisses that followed, I knew we could. For the first time ever the word Love passed between us. We went back to the pavilion and danced the evening away.

We had exciting news to bring back to Marg and Bill, but found them sleeping when we returned. I slept little that night for I had a lot of thinking to do. I felt that I would be taking a turn away from my life- long dream of a writing career. Since about the third grade, teachers had been assuring me that God had given me a gift of an inborn talent for writing. One principal, Miss Mathews, had called me to her office when I was in sixth grade to tell me that it was my duty to hone my writing gift and pursue a literary career or I'd never be happy. My own father had been most proud and encouraging and had tried to help me. He had once said to me early in the summer when Phil was coming out to the house quite often, *"Eva, Phil is a nice lad and I like him, but if you marry him, you will never write!"* Truly, the idea of marriage had never been in the picture when this adventure was conceived.

Phil had many qualities that I admired. He possessed a

great deal of plain common sense that appealed to one who was prone to imagine and to dream. He was an excellent worker as I had heard when we both were at Shonk's. He was strictly honest and dependable. But most of all, he was witty and fun to be with.

Phil sitting in the brush.

His talents could have made him a fine actor, for he was such a perfect mimic that he actually became the character he portrayed to howls of laughter from his audience. Phil was inherently musical and, though untrained, could pound out anything one could hum on the piano. He knew songs, words and all, from the turn of the century or before. He was a splendid dancer and went regularly to Chicago's palatial ballrooms where the best jazz bands in the country often played. He had favorite partners as well. Phil had a trim figure, liked clothes, dressed well and was a nice looking blond type with very expressive, opal eyes that changed colors with the different shades he wore.

All of these were plusses, but I knew that he had no conception of my interests and the real me, and wondered if I could communicate them. In any case, he was a warm, sympathetic person and I loved him.

Two lovers on the Gandy Bridge.

All slept later on the next morning that was Sunday, November second. Our buddies called for pancakes and while they were cooking, Phil told Marg and Bill our news. They said they were happy to hear it but weren't surprised as they expected it all along! It did introduce some excitement, however, for we wanted to do it as soon as possible as all admitted that we were tired of camp life and of being vagabonds. The upshot was that we set November fifteenth, a Saturday, for the ceremony. Much had to be arranged in slightly less than two weeks!

We decided that we would make the wedding as simple and inexpensive as we could. There would be shopping to do, a license to buy, a judge to see and parents to notify. We would say nothing to the Rouschs as we felt that they were under the impression that we were two married couples. Discussions continued all day.

We thought we would enjoy a boat trip across the Bay to St. Petersburg. The Gandy Bridge was under construction, the longest in the country at that time, but it wouldn't be opened until some months later. We would need a wedding ring, but I insisted not an engagement one at that time.

Phil and I went back to the dance pavilion that night to dance and to romance a bit, but mostly to plan. Marg and Bill were returning from their outing as we arrived around ten. We were about to turn in, dressed as usual, when Bill turned to me and, with mischief in his arresting light-flecked blue eyes, said, *"Eva, you now have my permission to sleep beside Phil.* "So, Marg and I moved to the center and the boys took to the outsides. Now we all could sleep in the arms of loved ones.

A change of pace began on Monday, November third. Fred Rousch had contracted for five houses in Pierce, Florida, so we packed the Liz and drove the fifty miles to an absolute wilderness area. We learned that the town was practically owned by a phosphate magnate and his company controlled that everything there. Practically the only building

Florida Bound Vagabonds

was a small hotel for the workers.

The area was so wild and overgrown that Bill and Phil said that even they would be afraid to stay there in a tent. The alternative was to drive back to Sulphur Springs. Fred lent us his truck and Bill and Marg went back in it while Phil drove the Liz. It was nearly nine that night when we reached *"home"* and made late supper.

All up at five the next morning to get the boys off in time to arrive in Pierce by eight, after they left, the day began to drag for Marg when the chores were finished. I had writing to do so no time to be bored, ever. She rounded up things to wash and did them. In those days, radio was just beginning to make itself known. Phil's uncle's company, Nagel Chase, had begun to manufacture some portable receivers with ear phones and Phil had brought a few along hoping to sell them, but there were no relay stations to speak of. Marg loved to read but had run out of material. A trip to town was indicated and we got into our dresses.

I knew that Mrs. Rousch had a sewing machine and, since I had always sewed since about age fourteen, I got the idea to make a simple dress for my wedding. In 1924 we could buy silk by the yard quite reasonably as rayon and other synthetics had not been perfected yet. We wore real silk stockings or cotton ones.

In Tampa I bought three yards of silk Canton crepe in a cinnamon shade and a simple pattern. The dress would have a cream-colored lace collar, three quarter length sleeves and be of about calf length. I bought a small hat and new gloves to match. The outfit could be used for other occasions, also. Marguerite bought some embroidery material, a paperback book and some magazines.

When we returned, I spread the dress material on the clean canvas tent floor and cut it out. Had it pretty well basted by suppertime as Marguerite helped with the fitting. The next day Mrs. Rousch was pleased to allow the use of her sewing machine so I felt that it would be nicely finished by the time it was needed.

Marg and I felt quite safe alone, but as a precaution, we kept our only weapon, the hatchet, beside the bed at night. Of course, it was never needed. My days passed more rapidly than Marg's for I was busy writing. I had a story idea and Father's letters kept urging me to keep at it. I was to send my efforts to him for critique. Or course, I thought my family had been pretty lucky to have my diaries instead of sporadic letters. I also wrote them of my impending marriage.

On Friday, November seventh, we slept until eight o'clock. We had hoped the boys would arrive the night before, but had been disappointed. We had a routine day with the usual swim at the springs and by suppertime, when they hadn't appeared, we decided to eat. Then we sat outside in the twilight and had about given up when the Rousch truck came rattling up and there they were! The Rousch back door was thrown open and mom and kids rushed out. There were hearty welcoming embraces all around. We were quite a crowd with Fred and his two brothers, his wife and three kids as well as the four of us.

All talked at once, but we finally learned that the job was finished and they were delighted to get back to civilization, that they hated the food at the hotel and were eager for home-cooked meals. They said that they had eaten, *"Grits! Grits! Grits!* Brother Burt added, *"...when they had bacon, it was so thin you could read the Lord's Prayer through it!"* There was much fun and laughter and it was a real celebration.

Phil and Bill went to work on Saturday, but were back by noon. All decided on a trip to Tampa after lunch and a swim. Phil and I left first as we had business to accomplish. We had some serious conversations. Our decision had been sudden, but we felt that we knew each other better for having been cooped up constantly in each other's company for more than a month and had got along splendidly. There seemed no real reason why we should not take the final step.

Marg and Bill had been great chaperones and companions, but I knew that I would not have needed them, for there would have been no physical relationship without marriage. It was 1924 and mores on that subject were rigid as was my upbringing.

We also were considering that Marg and Bill deserved a break. We all had had an excellent relationship, but we felt sure that they needed to be alone, as we would.

That day Phil bought my wedding ring, the narrow white gold band with a bridal wreath design that was in vogue then. He worried that he didn't have an engagement ring, but I assured him that that could be bought at another time. *(It was, too, a lovely diamond and sapphire one for my birthday).* We had intended to pick up the license, but it was Saturday and the office was closed. We finished the afternoon at a movie and brought some bakery goodies home for supper.

Phil, Eva, Marg, Bill.

Nothing could be accomplished on Sunday and all slept late. If we had felt the need to attend church we could have gone to the nearby Baptist or Episcopal one a block away, or the Spiritualist Temple just behind us. By evening the air would be full of preaching so we had the benefit of a sanctified area at least!

Marguerite and I had been reared Catholic while Bill and Phil had Protestant backgrounds and all were non-practicing. The boys had named the small building behind us the *Spook Temple* and just contemplating that as moonlight filtered through the eerily draping Spanish moss at twilight, made it easy to imagine the passage of the spirits floating back to the temple!

The week sped by and the dress was nicely finished, clothes to pack were in order, the license had been purchased and the judge appointment made. His office was right there in Sulphur Springs. Phil did his packing after I ironed a couple of his shirts, an unusual duty for a bride-to-be!

Saturday morning, November fifteenth, broke fair and remained unusually beautiful all day. Fortunately, the boys didn't have to go to work. We slept late, ate a good breakfast, worked around the place until about eleven and went for a good swim. Had lunch afterward and then dressed.

Marguerite and Bill accompanied us to the office of the Justice in Sulphur Springs and were our witnesses as we took the vows at about two-fifteen. I think that Phil felt them as deeply as I did for I meant every word - forever! He put the little ring on my finger and I promised myself never to remove it. *(And I never have taken it off, even through swollen fingers during pregnancy or during bouts with hives. It has worn plain on the top side from rubbing against other rings, but the little bridal wreath design on the bottom is clear for all to see after sixty-four years!)*

We went immediately to the dock on Tampa Bay where we said good-byes to Marg and Bill and boarded the boat for the two-hour ride to St. Petersburg. (*We simply hadn't thought of flowers or wedding pictures and have regretted that.*)

We settled ourselves on deck as not too many passengers opted for that and sat close to the railing so as to watch the water creatures that included turtles as big as washtubs! The size of the Bay also surprised us. We were happy, but rather quiet as we attempted to realize and absorb the step we had just taken. It most certainly would change the course of our lives. I had two letters unopened in my purse and brought them out to read. One was from home with congratulations and a check and the other was from a lad who worked in the office where I had been employed, Les Piper. Phil knew him, too, so I read the letter aloud. It was just a friendly note, but my new husband showed a flash of jealousy that really surprised me. It took a bit of reassuring, but all was well when we docked at St. Petersburg some time after five.

We inquired the way to town and took a streetcar to the center. Then it was just a matter of walking along and choosing a hotel from several. We picked the Alexander and soon were settled in a nice room on the third floor.

It was difficult to describe our feelings on being back in civilization! We hadn't even seen a regular bed and furniture since we left home on October first. I plopped down on a chair and Phil took a dive at the bed on which he sprawled with joy. We settled our luggage, freshened up and set out to find a restaurant where we could leisurely enjoy a good meal. Afterwards, we walked about the downtown area to acquaint us with our surroundings and ended up seeing a movie starring Betty Compson at the Plaza right across the street from our hotel.

It was nearly midnight and even at this great age, I am embarrassed to reveal my complete innocence as to what was to transpire to let me in on the secret of the great sexual mystery! Most people with a Catholic background early in the century would agree that sex just wasn't discussed much in the home or at school or anywhere else. I had read French writers and great love stories, but never learned exactly what they did for this charge of ecstasy! I had never seen male anatomy, except that of babies or statues and paintings at the Art Institute and couldn't make the connection! Of course, the missing link was the little matter of erection!

I learned later that Phil had some misgivings; also, as it turned out that we both were virginal. The exploratory effort that was made that night was a sweet, compassionate and loving experience even if without the *"bells-ringing, lightning-flashes"* of ecstasy I had read about, because the act simply could not be completed due to a resistant hymen and a gentle lover who was reluctant to cause pain. We fell asleep happily on a comfortable bed, cozily wrapped in each other's arms, with the certain knowledge that the thrills would come.

Sunday was spent pleasantly with papers to read, card and letter writing, good meals to enjoy and just lounging in a comfortable, civilized room. What a great change from our traveling home! We made faces when we thought of it.

We strolled about town in the late afternoon and noted many tourist types as well as many elderly people and were amazed at the numbers of folks sitting on the benches that lined a lot of the streets. We had intended to see a movie after dinner, but found that theaters were not open on Sundays. Instead, we walked through a pretty park and finally ended the evening by standing with a crowd on the wide steps of a Protestant Church listening to the beautiful music of an excellent choir.

On Monday, we slept late, had breakfast in the hotel dining room and then set out to look at the shopping areas. We had the fun of discovering a circus parade in progress and stood with the crowd at the curbs to watch it. Nostalgia carried me back to childhood in Des Moines where we saw a big parade every year from the windows of Father's downtown office. After lunch we did more exploring and decided we liked St. Pete, as we heard it called.

Because of work, we had to get back to Sulphur Springs and planned to take the five-thirty boat. The new movie, *The Covered Wagon*, was showing at the Plaza, so we went in. We loved it, but it ran long and we had to leave before the end, reluctantly.

Most of the trip back to Tampa was made after dark and it was chilly although we still stayed on deck. Rather dreaded seeing the old camp so soon again as we boarded the trolley for Sulphur Springs. Marg and Bill were asleep when we arrived.

Next day we learned that they had been scouting for a place to rent and had found one that they thought might serve at least temporarily. They expected it to be vacant in a week or so.

That day Fred Rousch did some fretting about the slacking off of roofing orders. He had heard of work still available in St. Pete, of all things! Salesmen also were in demand there. When he heard that, Phil, who would try anything, decided to go at once and test his luck. He canvassed the town and came back after a few days to tell us that he had a week's work for a crew there.

Once again, we packed up and took to the road. I don't remember too much about that as I had discontinued daily note writing when we no longer toured. Phil and Bill and a local crew did the work and we camped nearby. One incident stands out. The men roofed quite a large house that was surrounded by huge pecan trees. One branch, loaded with those gorgeous big paper shell pecans projected over a section of the roof and the men loaded their pockets for all to enjoy. The home belonged to a sheriff who was saving that special tree for the Christmas sales and he was furious. He didn't arrest them, but did charge them fifteen dollars that they split four ways. Those were costly but mighty yummy pecans!

Back in Sulphur Springs, Phil had his sales commission plus his labor wages so felt quite flush. The rental house had been vacated and it was quite close to the Rousch's, so also within walking distance of the Fountain of Youth which was a plus. Actually, it was only a cut better than our camp, but would provide more comfort and privacy.

The house was a large one, set in a very big, partially fenced and weedy yard. Our rooms on one side of it, and with separate entrance, contained double beds, two chairs each and wardrobes, but little else. The windows on one side only were wide, screened, shuttered and without glass! Cooking facilities were on the broad back porch with overhang roof and consisted of a three-burner gasoline stove with portable oven, an old kitchen cabinet, a rickety oilcloth covered kitchen table along with four beat-up chairs. It certainly wasn't a palace!

Near the back porch was a guava tree under which sat a bench that held a washtub. There was a pump nearby and an outhouse some distance away. The place looked reasonably clean and would cost us twenty dollars a month to rent.

The old lady owner, Mrs. Baron, lived in the main house in the center and there was another such *"apartment"* on the far side with its own entrance.

We decided to move in, if only temporarily, as Marguerite and I still hoped to find work, though as it turned out, that was a forlorn hope. For the time being there was roofing work.

Practical Phil even suggested that he and I look for a lot to buy and we found an adjoining pair on the outskirts of Tampa for five hundred dollars. After a small down payment, they could cost only ten dollars a month.

Phil and Eva in front of the house.

So, again Marg and I were left to our own resources during the days. We still could shop at Rutger's and we provided good meals for our husbands. We also kept our quarters clean and tidy and the exterior somewhat improved. On washdays we pumped a tub full of water early and let it stand in the sun for a couple of hours until it was warm. Then it was scrubby-dub-dub on the washboard. We rinsed in cold water, although Florida water was never very cold.

We thought of sending home for our pre-packed trunks with clothing and other necessities. However, caution dictated delay until we found better quarters.

Mrs. Baron.

We had time to become acquainted with Mrs. Baron and I really enjoyed Marg's mimicry of her. I haven't mentioned that Marguerite had a fantastic sense of the ridiculous and was a gifted cartoonist with words rather than with drawings. She was a delight to be around when she got started and I have laughed until I couldn't see for tears at some of the exaggerated descriptions. Baron was a wonderful target. She called herself a, *"Georgia Cracker."*

She was short, fairly stout, with thin grayish hair drawn into a ball at the back of her head, rather plain-faced with freckles and yellowish skin, small shrewd, brown eyes set a bit close together, thin lips and strong chin.

She said that her daddy was Irish and that he had knifed more than one evil man in his day! If so, she seemed to have inherited some of his wicked instincts for she apparently had no use of anyone. She felt that everyone was out to *"do"* her and cackled maliciously when her so-called enemies were in trouble. She wished them harm of every sort! She told us she had no earthly use for churches for folks only attended services to cover their tracks. Ministers were the worst!

Yet, she was a bible fanatic. After cussing a bewildered bill collector out she would go to her room and we could hear her singing some hymn-like tune and shouting, *"Oh, Lord, I want to be with you in the sky!"*

It usually was giggle time for my sister and me. Strangely, she seemed to like us. The occupants at the far side of the house had their own entrance so we saw little of them.

They were a widow and her extremely retarded middle-aged daughter who was pathetic as she slobbered when she spoke. She had a pet parrot that could perch on her head or arm or any place it wished and she even kissed it on its beak. Her mother was pleasant but quiet and seemed to prefer keeping to herself.

We spent quite a happy winter and hardly felt the financial restrictions. We made friends and visited them. There were trips to Tampa to shop or to see a movie. We ate too many delicious oranges after visits to the packinghouse. I kept writing as Father urged me to do and sent him a short story to critique. He made some suggestions, but ended with, *"... but, by golly, Eva, it proves that you CAN WRITE!"* which was encouraging.

There was a memorable trip to the ocean with the Rousch's who knew of a good place to find oyster beds. I don't remember just which coast it was, but it took a while to get there. They had brought crisp, round crackers and some jars of hot sauce. Fred and his brothers had heavy gloves and would reach under the water to feel the ledges and bring up rocky pieces to which the oysters clung, crack them with a tool and pass them around to be placed on a cracker to be doused with sauce. They thought them delicious, but I wasn't eager to try the things, though I finally took one or two with plenty of hot sauce. The Rousch's were young and fun to be with, so we had a great day.

Bill, Marg, and Eva enjoying the Atlantic.

Phil and I continued to go dancing and, of course, Marg and I practically lived at the pool, often meeting interesting people. One such was the young wife of the Fire Diver who was performing in Tampa. He would leap from a very high platform, set himself afire and dive into a big tub of water below. She performed, too, but only seemed to know two or three fancy dives. The climate was great and we really loved

Florida.

However, the sense of financial insecurity was always present and it was confirmed in March when the roofing jobs ended. There seemed to be very few others, but our boys kept looking and finally found employment as posthole diggers for the telephone company, so swooped from the heights to the depths in more than one sense. The pay was miserably low and the work in snake-infested swamps was unbearable at times. Much as we wanted to stay, we began to think of going back to Illinois where we knew there was work.

Once again, we organized our traveling home. The motor was overhauled, but the tires looked sturdy. The cabinet and tent were set in place, groceries were stocked and the jobs were chucked.

It was two in the afternoon when we left our happy home of four months. Mrs. Baron and the Harrison's, widow and daughter, bade us farewells that fell little short of being tearful! We stopped at Rutger's store for gas and oil and Louis came out and shook hands, wished us well and told us to be sure to come again.

We had paved roads for forty miles and then struck terrible sand and dirt ones which continued until we put up at an abandoned tourist camp near Dunellon. It really was a wild and lonely looking place beside a river. The boys made a campfire of pine needles and wood. Before dark we saw thousands of ducks on the water. It was very hot and sticky and the giant mosquitoes were so bad that we had to use blankets for covering even our heads! We could hear curlews calling and the grunts of alligators in the river. It was just too uncomfortable to sleep and we passed time by discussing some of our adventures such as the one at Inverness when we noticed a Negro shack on fire. It was one of a cluster and the boys found buckets, quickly pumped them full and put out the fire. They saw only one little black boy and he said his mother was visiting!

After two or three hours of sleep we welcomed the ring of alarm at five, had a quick breakfast and broke camp in heavy rain. Some of the day was bright and we managed two hundred miles in spite of three flat tires. They'd looked good when we started out, but we figured the winter's salt air had dried them out. Proceeding North, rains nearly bogged us down and our generator failed so we couldn't drive after dark. Mornings were cold and cranking the motor by hand became a challenge. There was one problem after another and instead of chronicling them day-by-day, I feel it best to telescope the rest of the final week.

Phil and Bill changing a tire.

Florida Bound Vagabonds

The most direct route took us through Atlanta, Chattanooga, Nashville, Louisville, Indianapolis and Chicago. Some of the roads were terrible, but there were many good ones as well. We were ecstatic about the great beauty of the Cumberland Range and the drive over paved roads to Signal Mountain. We had a most strenuous ride to the top of Mount Eagle, one of the highest peaks in the Cumberland's, over crushed rock which was slippery and we really were frightened a time or two when it almost seemed that we must slip over the edge and crash a few hundred feet to the rocks below. We fell in love with that area in spite of driving difficulty and camped at a lonely spot with no conveniences that night.

April 11, 1925: (The last diary entry.) Oh, Lord! I wonder if this old Ford will ever make it home! Here we are stopped again! Have traveled only five miles from last night's campgrounds. The boys are putting a new bolt on the transmission case. We are leaking oil fast. Gee, we've had enough trouble in the last seven days to last us the next seven years! Ten of twelve flat tire, fan belt off, water in the gas, leaky radiator hose, burned out transmission band linings, dropped washer in transmission case, oil petcock left open and gallon of oil lost, nearly burned out a bearing, ran out of gas twice, had to take two hills in reverse, rain best part of four days resulting in soaked bedding that had to be discarded, slept on hard ground last night with only two quilts under us. Entire trip made without generator so no lights, no horn and no starter all of the way. Now we have a main bearing knock of some seriousness and wrist pin knock! Later: Doggone, stopped again! Oil leaked out so fast that new gaskets had to be put in the transmission case. Another delay, only 88 miles to Chicago. What next?

Well, we made it home at last! Yep, arrived at two in the afternoon. Everyone was here except Papa. He was on his way to Memphis where his mother, my grandma Eva, was dying! Sadness to greet us when we had counted so much on complete happiness, poor Grandma! Little did I dream that when she left here last summer, I would never see her again!

The fairy tale was over and we had grown up in many ways in spite of frustrations, or perhaps, because of them. Though at times in tight financial situations, we never felt poor. On the contrary, we felt privileged to stay perfectly healthy and to live in such a lovely area, doing all of the exciting things we wished, being in love and with loved ones. We had seen and appreciated a good part of our wonderful country, met countless interesting people, learned to cope with problems as they arose and remained a happy foursome who now faced the future with courage and optimism as adults.

END

Appendix

Expenses - Camping trip from Tampa, Florida to Chicago, Illinois, April 4th to April 11th, 1925 - about 1,400 miles.

Ap 4	83 miles	
Gas & Oil		$2.33
Ap 5	193 miles	
Inner tube		1.75
Razor blades		.40
Candy		.20
Ap 6	205 miles	
Gas		2.97
Oil		.20
Groceries		1.82
Candy		.10
Tire and tube		10.00
Ap 7	200 miles	
Gas		4.36
Oil		.65
Radiator hose		.25
Groceries		.93
Apples		.11
Ap 8	187 miles	
Gas		2.74
1 tire & shoe		8.50
Oil		1.65
Groceries		1.20
Bar-b-que pig		.40

Ap 9	190 miles	
Gas		1.44
Oil		.40
Groceries		.90
Toll bridges		.89
Candy		.25
Camphor ice		.15
Cigarettes		.90
Lamp chimney		.10
Ap 10	196 miles	
Gas & Oil		3.92
Inner tube		1.85
Groceries		2.13
Candy, nuts, pop		.40
Ap 11	101 miles	
Groceries		.83
Oil		1.00
	1,355 miles	$57.02

Evelyn Marie Costello-Rucker
(Evelyn Rucker)

www.ingramcontent.com/pod-product-compliance
Lightning Source LLC
Chambersburg PA
CBHW040801150426
42811CB00056B/1129